MAKING THE WRITING AND RESEARCH CONNECTION WITH THE I-SEARCH PROCESS

A How-To-Do-It Manual

Second Edition

Julie I. Tallman
Marilyn Z. Joyce

**HOW-TO-DO-IT MANUALS
FOR LIBRARIANS**

NUMBER 143

NEAL-SCHUMAN PUBLISHERS, INC.
New York   London

Published by Neal-Schuman Publishers, Inc.
100 William Street
New York, NY 10038

Printed and bound in the United States of America.

The paper used in this publication meets the minimum requirements of American National Standard for Information Sciences—Permanence of Paper for Printed Library Materials. ANSI Z39.48-1992. ∞

Library of Congress Cataloging-in-Publication Data

Tallman, Julie I., 1944-
  Making the writing and research connection with the I-search process : a how-to-do-it manual / by Julie I. Tallman and Marilyn Z. Joyce.— 2nd ed.
      p. cm. — (How-to-do-it manuals for librarians ; no. 143)
  Joyce's name appears first on the earlier edition.
  Includes bibliographical references and index.
    ISBN 1-55570-534-0 (alk. paper)
  1. Library orientation for high school students. 2. Information retrieval—Study and teaching (Secondary) 3. Report writing—Study and teaching (Secondary) 4. Critical thinking—Study and teaching (Secondary) I. Joyce, Marilyn Z. II. Title. III. How-to-do-it manuals for libraries ; no. 143.
  Z711.2.J8 2006
  025.5'678223—dc22
                                                      2005032473

To our students and our colleagues who have made this book possible through their patience and willingness to share their journeys.

We also dedicate this second edition to all I-Searchers who have used this text themselves or via their teachers and teacher-librarians. May they always have confidence in their researching process and their ability to find, evaluate, and apply information to their questions and inquiries.

CONTENTS

LIST OF FIGURES

FOREWORD

Julie Tallman and Marilyn Joyce have created an important resource for teachers and media specialists to use in teaching students the art of research. The I-Search process is designed to ensure that students have a "stake in the topic" which, in turn, generates internal motivation and true growth and learning.

As an educator of students with disabilities, I read the material in the second edition of *Making the Writing and Reading Connection with the I-Search Process: A How-To-Do-It Manual* with great excitement. There are many times when strategies used for general education students cannot be adapted for use in teaching students with mild disabilities. However, I-Search has individualized instruction built into the process. Students who excel in academics and writing, as well as students who have great difficulty in these areas, can both benefit from the I-Search process.

One of the most difficult tasks facing students with mild disabilities is developing the capacity to ask and answer questions that will encourage and require cognitive processing. The pre-search steps and strategies embedded in the I-Search process teach questioning techniques to students. During the pre-search phase of research, the creation of higher-order questions "allows the topic to choose the student" and focuses the research.

The authors have included a template for a pre-notetaking sheet which will be helpful to all students. This pre-notetaking strategy is similar to the KWL (what I know, what I want to know, and what I have learned) strategy used in many classrooms. It is an improvement, however, on KWL strategy in that the three columns include "what I know," "what I don't know," and "what I want to know." In KWL strategy, students rarely return to the "what I have learned" column to sum up the knowledge gained from the activity. But pre-notetaking strategy allows students to include questions they don't know and develop questions that they want to find answers to, which will guide their research and allow them to develop additional questions as they move through the process.

In a traditional research project, students begin by taking random notes on index cards and then try to fit those disjointed notes into a cohesive "paper." In I-Search, students read for general information before they ever begin taking notes. For students with mild disabilities, this is an important part of the process. Often our students lack the prior knowledge from which to build an organized research project. This phase allows students to become familiar with general terms related to their topic as well as gather a general knowledge of the topic. At the end of each class period in which students read for general information there is a time for reflection, which encourages students to think about what they have read in terms of what they want to know and to record those thoughts in a learning log.

During the entire process of research, students are given individual support through conferences with the teacher and media specialist. In addition, fixed in the process is the collaboration with peers in the accordion exercise as well as in other steps. Peers can often generate questions that will assist the student in making a decision about what he/she wants to find out. Peers also learn from each other during the sharing of information at the end of the process.

The final product in I-Search can be presented in many forms. Students can prepare papers written from first-person perspective, computer software presentations, oral presentations, photo albums, diaries, action plans, and other formats. All final products, no matter what the format, will have promoted critical thinking and will result in learning that remains with the student and transforms his thinking. The ability to choose a format that fits the topic, as well as the needs of the student, will indeed be of benefit to *all* students, including students with disabilities.

In today's world, reading is undoubtedly the most stressed academic skill in schools. Under the federal No Child Left Behind Act, all children are expected to read "at grade level" by the year 2013–2014. I-Search addresses the importance of reading by infusing the following scientifically based research practices into its process:

- monitoring,
- using graphic and semantic organizers,
- generating and answering questions,
- recognizing story structure, and
- summarizing.

The authors have created a versatile resource that will be beneficial to all teachers and media specialists. I-Search can be adapted to fit the needs of students from elementary school through graduate school. It can be modified for shorter research projects and can be used in content areas as well as in writing classes. It promotes collaboration among professionals and students. I-Search is a research process that *could have* been developed for students with mild disabilities rather than general education students; it is a highly individualized process that meets the needs of all students.

Gail Best
Project Manager
The Accountability and Assessment
for Students with Disabilities Project
The Florida Department of Education

PREFACE

In today's electronic world, asking a pupil to write a research paper always runs the risk of turning into a meaningless, passive "cut and paste" assignment. Frequently, these are exercises where students write about topics in which they have no personal investment, mine other people's thoughts and ideas, and reassemble information to meet the instructor's requirements. The I-Search process tosses out that tedious model and brings research to life. Originally developed in the 1980s by Ken Macrorie, to help students in his college freshman composition classes develop their writing skills, the I-Search process encourages a dynamic approach to research by first tapping the power of students to pursue inquiries in their own interests. The process proceeds with students mastering strategies: brainstorming and making questions to seek answers about their topics. Throughout the various stages (narrowing the topic, using information, presenting the product, and assessing the process) teachers and librarians promote innovative tactics and demonstrate corresponding practical tools, such as freewriting, webbing, outlining, charting, graphing, and notetaking. Students triumph as they hone their research skills and discover a newfound confidence in their writing ability.

Over the years, I-Search has transformed the research landscape, and the process has proved successful at every grade level. In 1997, we adapted it into a successful guide targeted at middle school and high school students with *Making the Writing and Research Connection with the I-Search Process: A How-To-Do-It Manual.* This new edition revises, updates, and expands the tried and tested basics in the first edition. In addition, this second edition:

- incorporates new lessons learned from more years of teaching the process;
- responds to the feedback and requests received from other instructors;
- looks at how the process has matured due to dramatic changes such as ever-increasing access to an expanding number of information resources;
- connects easily to mathematics, social studies, and other new curriculum content areas;
- responds to new standards of the No Child Left Behind federal legislation;
- places new emphasis on reading strategies; and
- offers downloadable material on a CD-ROM.

ORGANIZATION

Part I, "The I-Search Process," covers the entire research process from idea inception through research paper assessment. It contains 16 illustrative figures.

Chapter 1, "Making the Writing/Research Connection," compares various writing and research processes, examines the steps of the writing progression, reviews models of research methods, and links I-Search to today's most important information literacy needs.

Chapter 2, "Exploring I-Search," overviews a brief history of the process, how a topic "chooses you," pre-search, the search process, and the final product.

Chapters 3 through 6—"Starting the Process," "Narrowing the Topic," "Using Information," and "Presenting the Product and Assessing the Process"—looks at the actual work of I-Search. These expanded chapters introduce new and improved strategies and their corresponding tools, such as pre-notetaking, scaffolding learning, log journaling, double-entry drafts, reflective entries, peer editing, options for presentation, and more.

Part II, "I-Search Connections," contains three chapters, featuring seven figures, that explores the evolving role and positive effect of the process.

Chapter 7, "Developing I-Search Management Strategies," completely rewritten for the second edition, includes more detail on time management, teacher/librarian collaboration, peer support, and interventions with students during the process.

Chapter 8, "Linking I-Search and Curriculum Content Areas" is entirely new to this edition. This chapter shows how to adapt I-Search principles to specific subject fields. It includes a mathematics I-Search unit and provides valuable insight into the process by which the instructor linked to it.

Chapter 9, "Connecting I-Search to Reading," is one of the most important additions to this edition. It connects information text reading with I-Search as a way to help students become more conscious of incorporating good reading strategies into their research.

Part III, "I-Search Resources," features print and CD-ROM content. An annotated bibliography of selected resources appears in this book; the CD-ROM contains three sample papers, planning worksheets, and an assessment rubric.

The all-new companion CD-ROM also contains all the figures in the book—more than two dozen different tools featuring charts, strategies, outlines, templates, handouts, worksheets, and sample papers and journals. Instructors are free to use these materials as is or redesign them according to their individual needs. All individual resources are supplied in a downloadable format.

Making the Writing and Research Connection with the I-Search Process: A How-To-Do-It Manual, Second Edition is designed to be flexible and may be combined into one cohesive unit or used selectively to emphasize certain skills. Teachers or librarians can adapt I-Search for as short or as long a time period as they have.

We hope *Making the Writing and Research Connection with the I-Search Process* will ignite an enthusiasm to work with student researchers, and inspire confidence in the strategies that help them succeed. We hope that it offers the hands-on tools that make students enjoy research projects, and provides them with the satisfaction of recognizing their own unique research process.

ACKNOWLEDGMENTS

We wish to acknowledge and thank our many students and our teacher colleagues who have participated in I-Search projects and generously shared their learned wisdom, joys, and successes with us, well beyond our classroom doors or online classes. We would like to extend special thanks to Alice Thomas, former social studies teacher at Brewer High School, Brewer, Maine.

We also wish to acknowledge and thank our mentors, particularly Ken Macrorie and Nancie Atwell, who unknowingly have helped us develop our own I-Search understandings. Our appreciation goes to Gail Best, Project Manager for the Accountability and Assessment for Students with Disabilities Project funded through the Florida Department of Education and Dr. Ross J. Todd of Rutgers, The State University of New Jersey, for honoring us with their observations on the value of this book and the I-Search, as presented in their Foreword and Introduction.

INTRODUCTION

Making the Writing and Research Connection with the I-Search Process: A How-To-Do-It Manual, Second Edition is about the leading of learning in twenty-first century schools. Founded on the fundamental interconnected literacies of reading, writing, and language development, the leading of learning in twenty-first century schools explicitly focuses on providing the best learning opportunities for students in the context of the rich, complex, diverse, and conflicting information environments that our schools and their communities have become. The leading of learning is not achieved merely through access to extensive print and digital collections within the school, or access to vast networks of information beyond the school. Rather, it is achieved through the carefully planned, closely supervised instructional interventions of instructional partners, who provide meaningful learning experiences that develop students' competence with learning from a variety of sources, enabling them to build deep knowledge and deep understanding of curriculum content and, indeed, build personal, social, and cultural agency.

The American philosopher, educator, and psychologist John Dewey described learning as an active individual process—not something done to someone but rather something that a person does. Dewey posited that learning takes place through a combination of acting and reflecting on the experience and its consequences, what he called reflective experience or reflective thinking. Dewey saw learning as highly personal and individual, where the experience of the learner, critical inquiry, and ownership were essential to meaningful learning. He believed that education must engage with and enlarge experience, connect to the personal lives of the students, enlist their natural curiosity, be directed toward the investigation of matters of interest, and prepare them for work, citizenship, and living in a free and democratic society.

Many decades since Dewey made his important contributions to educational thinking, the information-intense educational landscape of the twenty-first century acknowledges the important cornerstones identified by him. These cornerstones form the basis of *Making the Writing and Research Connection with the I-Search Process*. One cornerstone is the development of intellectual agency, where students engage in intellectual exploration; think deeply about diverse ideas and experiences; deal with conflicting data and problematic information; willingly engage in higher-order flexible thinking which involves analysis, synthesis, evaluation, and problem-solving; think creatively and laterally; reason with carefully chosen evidence and use the complex language of the discipline to do so; develop personal perspectives; and engage in substantive discussion of ideas. Another cornerstone is the development of personal, social, and cultural agency, where students do not just learn to transform information into their personal knowledge, but, through engaging with the world of ideas, learn about themselves as individuals and as social beings in a multicultural world. They come to respect different values, cultural knowledges, and viewpoints; they develop social and ethical values, understanding how information can be used in negotiation and decision-making. And they develop self-confidence as they investigate and try new ideas and practices, and learn to think outside the box.

The realization of these cornerstones comes through quality teaching. It calls for carefully structuring the learning environment and developing authentic learning experiences that enable students to be intellectually productive; that give them choice, meaning, and relevance in the scope and direction of their learning, that support them in many ways, including instructional interventions targeted to the knowledge construction process. It is quality teaching that enables students to transition from learning to read and write to reading and writing to learn. Quality teaching is founded on the concept of partnerships, and central to the I-Search process are partner-leaders leading learning: classroom teachers integrate their knowledge and expertise of curriculum standards with the information-learning expertise of school librarians. The classroom dynamics of implementing the I-Search process are systematically and explicitly articulated, supported by examples, templates, worksheets, and handouts. These support students throughout their inquiry, dealing with affective, cognitive, and behavioral demands of the research task, and facilitating personalization and ownership of learning, connections to personal lives, the ability to link the narrative of the text to the narrative of the students' lives in meaningful, engaging, and productive ways.

Ross J. Todd
Center for International Scholarship in School Libraries
School of Communication, Information and Library Studies
Rutgers, The State University of New Jersey

Part I
The I-Search Process

1 MAKING THE WRITING/ RESEARCH CONNECTION

"The problem with school reports lies in our methods for assigning them. We need to put the emphasis where it belongs—on meaning—and show students how to investigate questions and communicate their findings, how to go beyond plagiarism to genuine expertise and 'a coming to know.'" (Atwell, 1990, p. xiv)

The I-Search is an inquiry-based process, concentrating on questions that focus the research.

Sounds of moans and groans permeate the room as soon as students hear the dreaded words: "Class, we have a research project this term." Some middle school and high school—even college—students feel anxiety. Others view the research project as a waste of time. However, research projects are a primary tool for teaching information and technology literacy, as well as content learning. With the I-Search, library media specialists and teachers can transform the research project into a positive experience for students. It can become one of the most intense and authentic learning experiences in an academic program.

How do students become motivated to conduct their research enthusiastically? As it is now, most students quit their research as soon as they think they have fulfilled what the teacher wants. The quality of their products equals the power of external motivators, such as grades. Researching for the teacher, rather than for themselves, increases the likelihood that their new collection of facts will not generate authentic learning growth. As a result, many of the products that teachers receive at the end of a research assignment reflect students' lack of enthusiasm and motivation. The writing is frequently stilted due to lack of topic focus and obvious compilation of facts, seemingly without relationship to ideas or synthesis. The increased student tendency to copy and paste from the Internet material which they have not evaluated or synthesized for its applicability to their topic becomes obvious to the reader.

Daniel Callison (2000) purports that "motivation helps to increase the chances that students will learn what is needed even when they may initially classify the activity as being overly demanding or of no interest" (p.1). Many students may greet the announcement of a research assignment with negativity, nonetheless, if teachers can create a research experience that generates internal motivation, as well as the traditional external motivation, they will observe more permanent student learning; growth.

Teachers today have less time than ever to monitor student research, yet monitoring is more critical now with Internet access to billions of information sources, through effective search engines. When teachers assign research topics that do not require solving a problem or synthesizing information to answer a question, students in all likelihood will routinely collect and paste together a plethora of facts on a topic that probably is essentially meaningless to them and/or will not have a place in their long-term memory. They have not invested in critical thinking that would generate ideas and enhance their own perspective on the topic. Yet, students expect and receive As for their work. When this happens, they escape the assignment without producing a response to their research that demonstrates a higher-order level of understanding.

Students in English or language arts classes bring a sense of individual voice to their narratives and creative papers. When it comes to research assignments, however, one of the inevitable problems is that they do not know how to make the transition from other authors' voices to their own.

"And writing in the content areas does not have to fit a format that does not exist in the real world of nonfiction prose." (Atwell, 1990, p. xii)

One possible solution to this problem would be for students to generate personal interest through creation of their own questions about the topic. Students connect to topics that pique their interests. As it is now in American schools, students have very little opportunity to practice the critical art of question-making. If teachers choose to include higher-order question-making in a research assignment, in most cases, they would need to introduce strategies to scaffold or support their students with the skill. Thus, when teachers lack time within the curriculum, many assign topics instead of having students create questions about the content they are studying. Yet, when students work with a general topic without a question, it usually results in a lack of focus for their research and a lack of enthusiasm for extending interest in the topic beyond the minimum. Their goal is to do what the teacher asks, resulting in learning only what they think the assessment requires. Very seldom do students display obvious pride and ownership in their work.

"Writing questions was another way that students focused attention on and generated information." (Thompson, 1990, p. 41)

Students often try to find much of what they need by "Googling" their topics. However, if they create interest in a topic by generating their own questions, they will look for information that answers those questions, instead of spending a lot of time guessing about the information they truly need. The key is to help them invest in the topic through strategies like brainstorming and question-making. If invested, students will concentrate their information search on what they want to find out. The I-Search supports their interests by using a number of strategies to keep students focused on that interest, such as reflective journaling.

What strategies and techniques can media specialists and teachers use to overcome the obstacles that lead to such poor quality research writing? When a student writes, the student learns. But if students borrow so heavily from others, whether from the Internet or other sources, when do they have a chance to learn from their writing, if their writing is essentially someone else's?

The I-Search[1] process addresses this problem by integrating strategies that first promote question-making about a topic at the beginning of the research project and then encourage students to polish those questions as they get deeper into their research. The I-Search process melds the research process with the writing and reading processes.

Curriculum guides and school media literature demonstrate a number of parallels between the writing and research processes. Too often, media specialists and teachers do not consciously emphasize writing as part of the research process until the final product is prepared. But more productive learning growth happens when students research topics through their chosen essential questions. I-Search strategies emphasize the powerful connections between the research and writing processes, with reading strategies that enable the other two processes.

COMPARISON OF THE WRITING AND RESEARCH PROCESSES

The writing process, as defined in the English and language arts guides, and the research process, as outlined in information literacy guides, have a number of common characteristics. Writing and research both emphasize process. Both stress similar goals and objectives, employ many of the same teaching strategies, and take a similar approach to assessment. *Merriam-Webster's Collegiate Dictionary* (2003) defines *process* as "a series of actions or operations conducing to an end" (p. 990). Process is the means by which English and language arts teachers and media specialists move students from the status of beginning investigators to that of accomplished researchers, from beginning writers to authors.

Classroom teachers whose students write research papers and media specialists both want the writer or researcher to:

- interpret,
- analyze,
- synthesize, and
- evaluate information informing their topics.

Both assist students in moving through the processes for writing and research by teaching them the techniques of observing, brainstorming, freewriting, webbing, outlining, charting, graphing, and

"Brainstorming is a particularly effective strategy for remembering and retrieving information and for quickly getting down on paper a quantity of related ideas." (Thompson, 1990, p. 42)

"We like to say that we send children to school to teach them to think. What we do, all too often, is to teach them to think badly, to give up a natural and powerful way of thinking in favor of a method that does not work well for them and that we rarely use ourselves." (Holt, 1983, p. xi)

notetaking. Finally, both assess process and product during the activity as well as at the end of the experience. In spite of these similarities, there are major omissions in each process. Each rarely contains references to the other discipline's research and process models. For example, most English and language arts curriculum guides fail to reflect current trends and practices within the research process.

The school media profession does not have consensus on a common research process model, whether it is fitting linear process steps to a research topic or using an iterative, nonlinear process focusing on questions arising from a research topic. All the research process models have value if teachers and media specialists are cognizant of how and why they are choosing particular ones to teach their students. Each process bonds with the writing process in its own way. If the teacher's goal is a product, one type of process might be more efficient and faster than another. If the goal is transformative learning, in which embedded thinking and practices are challenged to facilitate changes, then a process that addresses that goal should be used. Logical reasons exist for the use of different models for different goals. Alternatives are available, including borrowing strategies from one process model to enhance another process model. One size does not fit all uses anymore, just as one teaching style does not fit all students' learning needs.

The I-Search process emphasizes a nonlinear approach to research. It can be messier and take more time than the linear, step-by-step routine that gets to a product faster. The I-Search process concentrates on students creating their own ideas and perspectives through their question focus and reflective activities. It is an inquiry-based process, using higher-order critical thinking about research, which offers multiple benefits for students. Inquiry-based learning is governed by a driving question and incorporates collaborative questioning and support for the other strategies as the students research and develop their final product. Higher-order critical thinking in the I-Search includes thinking at the levels of comprehension, evaluation, synthesis, and application of information to the question or problem.

Historically, the process approach to teaching writing has existed for several decades, but the process approach to teaching research is fairly new and published mainly in school media literature. The I-Search process model directly connects the research process to the writing process within the curriculum standards.

Recently, Stanley Wilder (2005) defined the academic library's de facto premise of information literacy as "a rigorous program of instruction in research or library-use skills, provided wholly or in part by librarians" to help students manage the information on the Internet (p. B13). Wilder contends that academic librarians want to make students into information seekers like themselves, which he claims, is "the wrong solution to the wrong problem" (ibid.). In his view, the current concept of information literacy assumes that the typical college freshman

> accepts unquestioningly the information she finds on the Internet, when we know from research that she is a skeptic who filters her results to the best of her ability. Information literacy tells us that she cannot recognize when she needs information, nor can she find, analyze, or use it, when she demonstrably does all of those things perfectly well, albeit at a relatively unsophisticated level (p. B13).

Instead, Wilder thinks that librarians should scaffold (i.e., a framework for supporting your students with the skill) students at the writing process stage. The effect would be to help students improve themselves as readers and writers within their discipline by using discipline-specific information. Wilder's comments imply the need for assistance with finding information that helps to shape questions generated about topics within the students' disciplines. Librarians would scaffold students in writing about how the information directs their questions, creating a higher level of learning in their discipline.

Wilder gives pre-collegiate level teachers and media specialists credit for creating satisfactory information finders who can analyze information and use it, but in an unsophisticated manner. The I-Search answers the "unsophisticated" characterization by connecting the research process with the writing process at the K–12 level, thereby strengthening both processes.

The I-Search writing and research relationship suggests the essential questions that serve as the premise for this book.

- How would teachers and media specialists use the relationship between the research and writing processes to help each student develop an effective research process?
- What is the connection between reading and the writing process?
- How can effective instruction in reading strategies improve reading comprehension and lead to better interpretation and evaluation of information, as well as improve writing?
- What is the role of the research process in improving the writing process within a content area?

- How do teachers and media specialists support students' writing within their research process?
- What is the ultimate goal of K–12 research and writing?

That goal should be the ability to express in writing a student-owned, critical perspective on how ideas, thoughts, and facts inform an essential question.

THE WRITING PROCESS

From the emergence of the writing process approach in the mid-seventies, language arts and English teachers developed a consensus that the writing process consists of five basic steps: pre-writing, drafting, revising, editing, and publishing.

STEP 1: PRE-WRITE

During this stage, students use a variety of strategies to select topics and generate supporting details. Some examples of pre-writing techniques include, but are not limited to: brainstorming, jot-listing, freewriting, reading, notetaking, and outlining. Students at this stage articulate their ideas by sharing their plans with classmates. Frequent conferences between student and teacher or media specialist facilitate essential progress at this and other stages of the process. The teacher and media specialist pose questions to stimulate critical thinking and help students overcome potential problems.

STEP 2: DRAFT

Ideas generated through prewriting pour onto the page as students write a rough draft. After creating a draft, students share their writing with each other, frequently in small groups of three or four. Their peers respond to drafts by posing questions for the writer and offering suggestions. While students share their drafts with members of their writing groups, teachers meet with individual students. During this conference, the student and teacher discuss what they like and dislike about the draft and consider possibilities for revision.

STEP 3: REVISING

Students use the input from peers and teacher to begin the third stage of the process, which is revising. During the revision stage, students add supporting details, eliminate nonessential information, reorganize thoughts, and clarify wording. Students receive input from peers and teacher, usually on an "as needed" basis.

STEP 4: EDITING

The fourth step occurs after one or more revisions of the composition. Students look closely at each line of text, make more refined changes in wording, and reorganize information where needed. Editing also includes proofreading the composition for errors in spelling, mechanics, grammar, usage, and sentence structure. Teachers seize the occasion of these errors to clarify grammatical concepts.

STEP 5: PUBLISHING

Publishing occurs when students share their writing with others. Reading finished papers to the class, posting compositions on a class Web site, bulletin board, or Internet blog, and creating a class literary magazine, either via print or Internet, are just a few of the many methods of publishing student writings. Sharing writing in this way brings the bonus of increasing students' self-esteem.

THE TRADITIONAL RESEARCH APPROACH

One discovery from a study of English and language arts curriculum guides is quite surprising. Some schools adopt a process model, while others concentrate on the specific information literacy and writing objectives included in the new national and state curriculum standards and performance indicators.

Many teachers and media specialists specialize in the linear form of the research process, including the following eight steps:

- **Step 1:** Choosing and limiting a topic. During this step, the teacher conferences once or twice with students, who then share their proposed topics with peers. Each student also creates a preliminary thesis statement for his/her topic.
- **Step 2:** Encouraging students to plan for the project by surveying resources, developing a bibliography and a preliminary outline, and sometimes composing questions to guide the research.
- **Step 3:** Reading and notetaking. Students create a pack-

age of notecards, which are graded and commented on by the teacher.

- **Step 4:** Revising the preliminary outline. Teachers check the outline and provide helpful comments.
- **Step 5:** Writing rough drafts. Teachers scan the drafts and comment on major weaknesses.
- **Step 6:** Revising returned drafts.
- **Step 7:** Creating a word-processed product and editing final manuscripts.
- **Step 8:** Submitting completed paper.

MODELS FOR RESEARCH AS A PROCESS

While writing teachers have come to a consensus on what constitutes the educational writing process, media specialists still use a variety of models for teaching the process of research. These models vary in terminology and the number of steps. Among the more than 100 models available through the Internet, Kuhlthau's *Information Seeking Process* (1993) was the first model in the library literature that is based on research. She established a close link between the two processes with her use of Emig's (1971) study of twelfth-grade English students as a springboard for her research. While Emig focused on information already known, Kuhlthau stressed "composing from what we learn from information" (p. xix).

Kuhlthau used the same methodologies in her studies that educational researchers employ with process writing. She analyzed student journals containing students' reactions to and feelings about their work. She interviewed or held conferences with students and conducted case studies tracing individual student behavior. More than isolating steps of a process, she investigated the metacognitive activities of students during the process, concentrating on feelings that evolved during research projects. Kuhlthau suggested a crossover between the writing process and the research process through her work.

Kuhlthau's research has a number of implications for this work and generates new questions. How do journaling and interviewing demonstrate the relationship between writing and research? Might student journals be more than a means of gathering and analyzing data for research? Could journaling be a strategy for helping students develop critical-thinking skills by having them reflect on their personal research process?

"Learning logs [journals] played a significant role in helping my students remember. Through prompts, I invited students to delve into their memories, to write what they already knew, and to appreciate their prior knowledge." (Thompson, 1990, p. 44)

Some research process models seem to underemphasize the important connection between the writing process and research process. However, Macrorie's (1988) I-Search appears to be the best tool for connecting the reading, writing, and research processes. The I-Search focuses on what students do with their information-finding.

The writings of Donald Murray (1982) further connect the writing and research processes. He provides the critical link by defining writing in terms of information processing. Murray's model of the writing process consists of the interaction of four forces:

- collecting,
- connecting,
- writing, and
- reading one's writing as part of the act of revising.

Here again is the emphasis on information-finding through collecting. The student connects what he/she finds by writing about it. According to Murray, people hunger for information: "Information, brought to us through sight, hearing, touch, taste, smell, is stored, considered, and shared. Our education extends the range of our information-collection through reading and research that reaches back in time and across the barriers of distance and difference" (p. 22). Wilder's (2005) view of post-secondary students as "apprentices in the continuous cycle of reading and writing" (p. B13) echoes Murray's words. The same connection can be made for K–12 students. According to Murray,

> We are compelled to provide some order for the confusion of information or it will drown us. We must discriminate, select the information that is significant, build chains of information which lead to meaning, relate immediate information to previous information, project information into the future, discover from the patterns of information what new information must be sought. The connections we make force us to see information we did not see before. The connections we are making also force us to seek new, supporting information; but, of course, some of that information doesn't support—it contradicts. So we have to make new connections with new information which in turn demands new connections (1982, p. 22).

Murray's analysis of writing as information processing adds a further dimension to the possibility of the I-Search as a research/

writing process. The process writing techniques and strategies are useful in the stages of the research process. Murray demonstrates how to move beyond process by showing people how to make meaning of information by tracing the evolution of thinking through the stages of writing and research. How does the researcher make connections from the information gathered? What role does writing play as the researcher moves through the stages of the research process? How can writing demonstrate the critical thinking at each stage of the process so that others can see where the researcher has been? Wilder's proposal should extend to the connection between the research and writing processes. If librarians desire to help students become readers and writers in their discipline, then the process they teach must make those connections and not be isolated to information literacy skills and strategies. The same applies to K–12 media specialists and their attempt to help students create their own successful reading/research/writing process.

The process models for both writing and research provide a foundation for development of a research process that connects with the writing process. Students must develop a successful research process that they easily and intuitively apply to new information problem-solving situations. Recalling Murray's words, "In teaching the process we have to look, not at what students need to know, but what they need to experience" (1982, p. 25). The traditional approach to the research paper is not the answer. The next chapter discusses the authors' adaptation of Macrorie's *I-Search Paper* (1988) for use as a research process.

NOTE

1. The I-Search process was originally developed by Ken Macrorie for his college freshman composition classes to help students develop their writing skills. This book presents an adapted version of the I-Search as a research/writing process that focuses on higher-order critical thinking skills, to build information literacy as well as writing skills.

REFERENCES

Callison, D. (2000). "Key instructional term: Motivation." Retrieved August 1, 2005, from http://www.crinkles.com/keyWords.html

Emig, J. (1971). *The composing process of twelfth graders.* NCTE Research Report No. 13. Urbana, Ill.: National Council of Teachers of English.

Holt, John. (1983). *How children learn.* Rev. ed. New York: Da Capo Press.

Kuhlthau, C. C. (1993). *Seeking meaning: A process approach to library and information services.* Norwood, NJ: Ablex.

Macrorie, K. (1998). *The I-Search paper.* Rev. ed. Portsmouth, NH: Heinemann.

Merriam-Webster's Collegiate Dictionary. (2003). 11th ed. Springfield, MA: Merriam-Webster.

Murray, D. M. (1982). "Writing as process: How writing finds its own meaning." In Murray, D. M. *Learning by teaching: Selected articles on writing and teaching.* (pp. 17–31). Portsmouth, NH: Heinemann.

Thompson, A. (1990). "Thinking and writing in learning logs." In Atwell, N. *Coming to know: Writing to learn in the intermediate grades.* (pp. 35–51). Portsmouth, NH: Heinemann.

Wilder, S. January 7, 2005. "Information literacy makes all the wrong assumptions." *Chronicle of Higher Education, 51*(18), p. B13.

2 EXPLORING I-SEARCH

ORIGIN OF THE I-SEARCH

In his book, *The I-Search Paper* (1988), Ken Macrorie, a university professor, laments, "For many decades high schools and colleges have fostered the 'research paper,' which has become an exercise in badly done bibliography, often an introduction to the art of plagiarism, and a triumph of meaninglessness—for both the writer and the reader" (Preface). His response was the "I-Search paper," which he created to improve the quality of his students' writing.

What is the I-Search research/writing process and how is it different from traditional research? Macrorie's definition of the I-Search is simple and direct: "A person conducts a search to find out something he needs to know for his own life and writes the story of his adventure" (Preface). In other words, not only does the "I" refer to the personal nature of the topic, but it also refers to the story, which takes the form of a first-person narrative. Macrorie explains the difference between the I-Search and the traditional research paper:

> I have been challenging students to do what we call *I-Searches*—not Re-Searches, in which the job is to search again what someone has already searched—but original searches in which persons scratch an itch they feel, one so marvelously itchy that they begin rubbing a finger tip against it and the rubbing feels so good that they dig in with a fingernail. A search to fulfill a need, not that the teacher has imagined for them, but one they feel themselves . . . (Preface).

Macrorie eloquently explains the problem with traditional research. The research process is an integral part of daily living. It presents itself in both simple and complicated forms. The weather report dispenses the data needed to decide how to dress. Buying a car means questioning salespeople, searching the Internet, reading *Consumer Reports* and automotive magazines, and asking friends about their satisfaction with their vehicles. A serious illness requires questioning doctors, seeking a second opinion, and searching the Internet for information about the illness to make

The traditional high school research paper re-searches what other people have already searched.

15

informed decisions. What a contrast this is to the traditional research paper, which, as Macrorie notes, is frequently a summary of secondhand information on topics that fail to engage students throughout a lengthy process.

Why teach students to research and write long, boring drafts unreadable to anyone? Why insist that the traditional research process, generating its voluminous notecards and written in third-person format, is the only acceptable process for students? Does the traditional process produce papers that contain evidence of well-thought-out arguments about ideas or investigations of problems? More frequently, these papers display evidence of facts to satisfy a page and source requirement. The papers evolve, often, from what the student thinks the teacher might want.

Usually absent is evidence of critical thinking resulting in a new perspective on the topic. Why? Think about the awkwardness of expressing ideas, when the writers have to start with, "This person thinks that . . . " Who teaches students the art of reflecting on their reading and focusing on questions about the subject matter? What if students could recount their thinking in the first person, probing their own thoughts about the questions? Students damage their integration of a successful research process when the traditional research process, at the K–12 level, encourages them to paste together others' ideas. Without the students' critical thinking melding the information and ideas into some kind of sensemaking form, their results will neither contribute to their own perspective nor give them an opportunity to reflect on the research and its implications for learning.

Is the I-Search the answer to these problems? With modifications, it would be a strong tool for teaching the research process, at the K-12 level? Donald Murray's (1982) model of writing as information processing connects together reading, new information, prior experience, knowledge of the research process models, and critical thinking. Application of these concepts to Macrorie's I-Search writing process results in the following adaptation of the "I-Search.

A TOPIC CHOOSES YOU

An initial chapter of the *I-Search Paper* (Macrorie, 1988) highlights the concept of a research topic choosing the researcher. To make research meaningful, a student has to have a stake in the topic. Macrorie states, "No one can give other persons knowledge, make them think or become curious. Knowledge must reside in a person or it is not knowledge; and even if that person accumulates it, without use it is—what else could it be—useless" (p.14).

One answer to the problem of making research meaningful is to encourage students to write about issues and problems that truly affect their lives. Think about the times in media centers when students and teachers have an immediate need for information. Their information needs range from the mundane to life-threatening: "I need to find a way to store all my junk. Do you think the Internet would have some information on closet organizers?" "My brother's just been diagnosed with Hodgkin's disease. My parents are really upset. Will you help me find some information on the Internet?" These people devour the available resources. They want to share what they are learning and their plans for using that information. Moreover, their stories are fascinating, as well as the outcomes of their searches. The question then becomes, "Why not incorporate that immediacy into a research assignment to make it meaningful?"

Macrorie (1988) suggests a novel proposition that applies to students: "What should *you* choose to search? I can't say enough times that this is the wrong question. Rather ask, 'What's choosing me? What do I need to know? Not what I believe will impress others, but what keeps nagging me?'" (p. 71). These make sense. Most teachers who assign research projects will have students who pick topics for the wrong reasons: "I think I'll write my paper on abortion. There's lots of information on the Internet, so I won't have problems finding information." "I'm doing outsourcing of jobs. Mr. Adams is always harping on it. That topic will impress him." Or the worst-case scenario: "My history teacher had us draw topics out of a hat for our research papers. I got 'the use of steroids in baseball.' I don't have any interest in sports, much less steroids, and don't know where to start!" Macrorie's comments are reminders about what is wrong with assigned research topics, even when there is plenty of room for choice within the parameters of the assignment. To be meaningfully integrated into the research process, the student's topic must arise from the student's *need* for information; especially information that could be useful in his/her life. To generate interest in a content area topic, the student must have the opportunity to turn the topic into a higher-order question that motivates him/her.

> The student's topic must arise from the student's *need* for information.

THE I-SEARCH FORMAT

K–12 teachers and media specialists' experiences with student research sound very similar to Macrorie's (1988) lamentation: "Other teachers and I have given so many instructions to students about form and length of papers that we've destroyed their natural curiosity. They don't want to grab books off the shelf and taste them" (p. 55). Unfortunately, this is the common scenario at the middle school and high school levels. Where is the approach to research that communicates excitement when the student finds information that solves a problem or contributes to decision-making? Macrorie's (1988) format of the I-Search narrative seems to meet the need:

1. What I knew [and didn't know about my topic when I started out].
2. Why I'm writing this paper. [Here's where the real need appears: the writer demonstrates that the search may make a difference in his life.]
3. The search [story of the hunt].
4. What I learned [or didn't learn. A search that fails can be as exciting and valuable as one that succeeds] (p. 64).

Figure 2.1 depicts the flow of the I-Search.

Figure 2.1. Flowchart: The I-Search Process

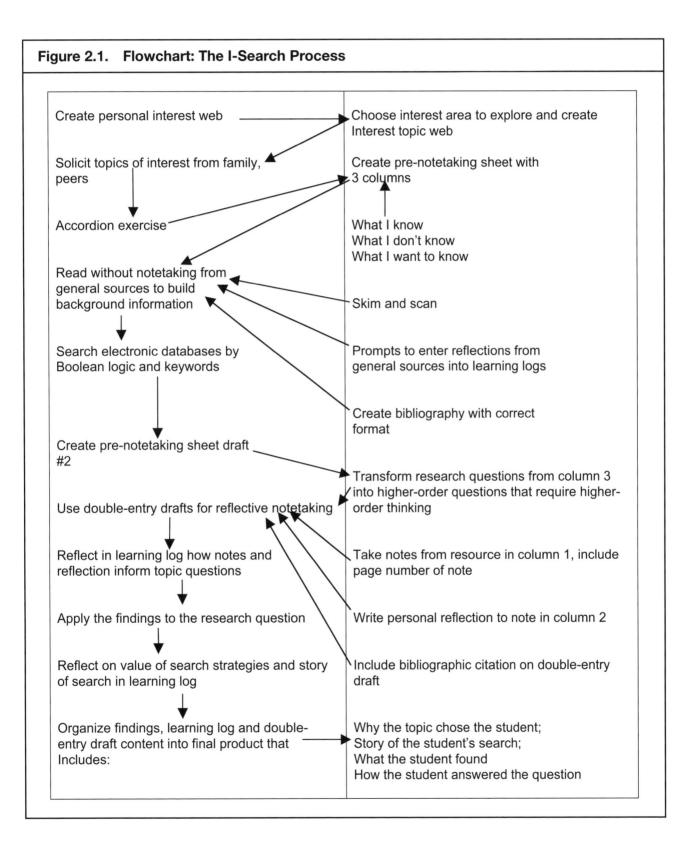

Create personal interest web → Choose interest area to explore and create Interest topic web

Solicit topics of interest from family, peers

Create pre-notetaking sheet with 3 columns

Accordion exercise

What I know
What I don't know
What I want to know

Read without notetaking from general sources to build background information

Skim and scan

Search electronic databases by Boolean logic and keywords

Prompts to enter reflections from general sources into learning logs

Create bibliography with correct format

Create pre-notetaking sheet draft #2

Transform research questions from column 3 into higher-order questions that require higher-order thinking

Use double-entry drafts for reflective notetaking

Take notes from resource in column 1, include page number of note

Reflect in learning log how notes and reflection inform topic questions

Apply the findings to the research question

Write personal reflection to note in column 2

Reflect on value of search strategies and story of search in learning log

Include bibliographic citation on double-entry draft

Organize findings, learning log and double-entry draft content into final product that Includes:

Why the topic chose the student;
Story of the student's search;
What the student found
How the student answered the question

CONCERNS ABOUT USING THE I-SEARCH PROCESS

If high school teachers question the use of a narrative format to report research, ask them if a narrative that exercises critical thinking skills needed for more complex forms of writing would be valuable. Macrorie (1988) thinks it would: "We often talk or write our way into understanding, especially when we tell a story of human action: relating how and where it happened often shows us why, and with what significance" (p. 99).

Murray's (1982) model also comes to mind. Writing about experiences forces the author to process thoughts about the topic. It gives the author something to return to and reflect on. It enables the author to make new connections as the author reads about others' experiences. The author begins to recognize cause and effect and evaluate events. Macrorie (1988) told his students: "The I-Search project is designed to give you lifetime skills in listening, interviewing, reading, quoting, reporting, and writing in a way that others will profit from and enjoy" (p. 71). The student learns and profits through the experience, not only about his/her topic question but also about the research strategies that are successful for him/her.

Macrorie's I-Search model clearly demonstrates the power of the narrative. The narrative can be a tool for meeting an information need, evaluating experiences related to that need, and deciding a future course of action. The development of stronger critical thinking skills is a natural consequence of entering into this process. Thus, the narrative speaks to a broader audience of readers and researchers. As Macrorie (1988) notes for his students:

> When you write a first-rate I-Search Paper, you'll not only be developing a useful lifetime habit and carrying out an intellectual task, but you'll also be getting experience in writing the sort of account often published in magazines and books these days. More and more, editors are ignoring the old essay and article forms. Readers are buying magazines and books which tell stories of experience rather than present reports that consist mainly of abstracted or generalized points and statistics accompanied by an anecdote or two (p. 77).

The I-Search paper is more than a vehicle for teaching the writing or research processes and more than a piece written for a

> Stronger critical thinking skills are a natural result of the I-Search experience. Critical thinking informs idea-making.

teacher or shared with fellow students in writing groups. The I-Search is a viable format suitable for publication.

THE I-SEARCH FORMAT AS A RESEARCH MODEL

> The I-Search merges writing and research throughout the process.

Macrorie (1988) presents a convincing argument for the use of the I-Search as a model for a combined research and writing process.

It has a format or steps that the authors merge with the stages of the thirteen-step research process, as outlined in the Maine model (Maine Educational Media Association's Ad Hoc Committee on Information Skills, 1990), which is representative of many versions of the research process. The Maine model was carefully crafted to synthesize a number of research processes available and, as such, constitutes a reasonably generic process. The stages of the pre-search phase of the Maine research process match easily with the first two stages of the I-Search paper, shown in Figure 2.2.

Figure 2.2. Flowchart: The First Two Stages in the I-Search Process

I-Search Format	Steps in the Pre-Search Process
What I Know	1. Formulation of the Central Research Question 2. Relation of the Question to Prior Knowledge (includes consulting broad resources such as general encyclopedias and general but evaluated Web sites) 3. Identification of Key Words and Names (includes skimming and scanning resources)
Why I'm Writing	4. Integration of Concepts Important to the Paper includes creating outlines, webbing diagrams, lists, and/or other organizational strategies) 5. Development of Questions to Guide Resources 6. (When Needed) Re-exploration of General Resources

Much of the success or failure of a research project hinges on the successful completion of the *pre-search* stage of the research process.

But is it a perfect match? Much of the success or failure of a research project hinges on the successful completion of the *pre-search* stage of the research process, demonstrated in Figure 2.3.

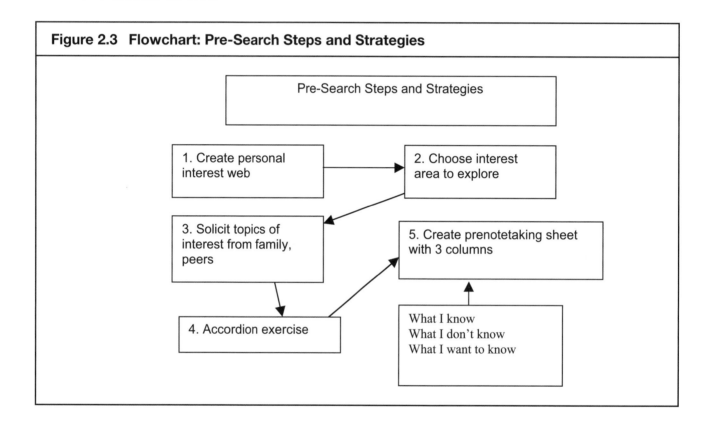

Figure 2.3 Flowchart: Pre-Search Steps and Strategies

Pre-Search Steps and Strategies

1. Create personal interest web

2. Choose interest area to explore

3. Solicit topics of interest from family, peers

5. Create prenotetaking sheet with 3 columns

4. Accordion exercise

What I know
What I don't know
What I want to know

Essential questions stimulate critical thinking.

At this stage, students select a topic, find a focus, write questions to guide their research, and create a tentative organizational pattern. Without these components, students lack direction and purpose, and are easily overwhelmed by a sea of information. The end result in such cases is frustration accompanied by the failure to complete the project or the creation of a paper consisting of numerous quotes strung together—the "cut and paste" approach to research. It is critical at this point to stress that the key to the rest of the process is the creation of essential questions.

These essential questions should be higher-order, critical thinking types of questions that begin with "how," "why," "which," or other words that indicate the student is questioning at a level that will require cognitive processing. The "how" question requires investigation of the process creating the problem. The "why" question demands a reason for the problem or topic question. The "which" question asks the student to compare and contrast two or more solutions to one or all the parts of the essential question(s).

The successful completion of the six steps listed in Figure 2.2 of the pre-search process is the first step toward a quality end product. Student creation of quality, higher-order essential questions focuses the search, allows other questions that spur investigation of various parts of the problem or topic, and makes room for essential fact gathering for decision-making.

What happens when Macrorie's two steps are added, and students select a personally meaningful topic? The result acts like a merger of the I-Search, Murray's (1982) model of information processing (collecting, connecting, writing, and reading), with Kuhlthau's (1993) model combining thoughts, actions, and feelings. The following steps emerge:

- Students keep a written record of their thoughts, actions, and feelings (Kuhlthau's model) as they move through the stages of a combination of Macrorie's format with the stages of the pre-search process.
- As they collect information by consulting general encyclopedias and skimming and scanning resources, including appropriate Web sites, students write about what they know and speculate on what they do not know about their topic.
- As they begin to establish and comprehend their motivation for researching their subject, students write about their information need.
- Students reread their drafts, share them with fellow students, their teacher, and the media specialist. Finally, they make revisions in their central research question and additional questions to guide their research.

The pieces fit. Murray's and Kuhlthau's combined theories merge successfully with Macrorie's vehicle for teaching the research process, as do the remaining concepts. Figure 2.4 represents an overview of the I-Search search process in graphic format.

Figure 2.4. **Flowchart: Search Process Steps and Strategies**

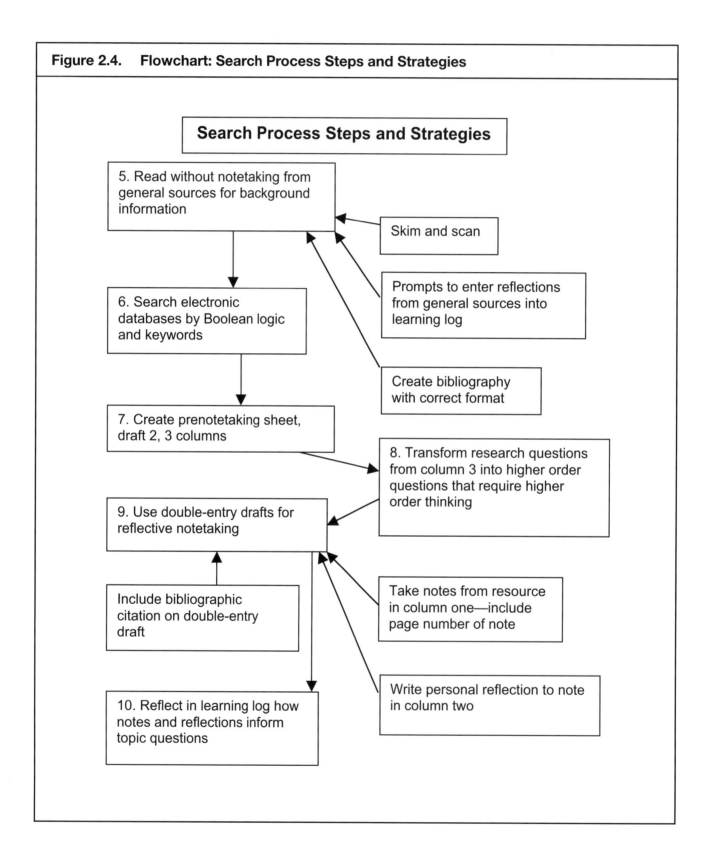

INTERVIEWING

In the next phase, Macrorie (1988) stresses the interview as a primary means of information gathering, in addition to the use of libraries. Furthermore, he advocates using dialogue from interviews in the I-Search paper's text. While this is an interesting approach to writing the I-Search, it may be too restrictive. Students need a broader variety of sources and strategies to develop and integrate within their own successful research strategies a wide range of information literacy skills that are omitted from Macrorie's explanation. The objective is for students to use writing as a tool that facilitates critical thinking and reflection about their thoughts and ideas.

Again, the Maine model guides a merger of information literacy strategies within the remaining phases of the I-Search. The relationships shown in Figure 2.5 then appear.

Figure 2.5. Map: Remaining Stages in I-Search Process	
I-Search Format	**Steps in the Research Process**
The Search (story of the hunt)	Search
	7. Locate Resources of Information
	8. Search for Relevant Information
	Interpretation
	9. Select and Evaluate Information (checking for currency, point of view, bias, author's/producer's motives)
	10. Interpret, Infer, Analyze, and Paraphrase (identifying main ideas, supporting details and opinions; relating content to the research questions)
	Application
	11. Organize Information for Applications (synthesizing information from sources, organizing it, and using an effective method of presentation)
What I Learned or Didn't Learn	12. Apply Information for Intended Purpose (making clear, well supported presentation; drawing conclusions based on information; evaluating the project and search process; being able to apply content and process to new learning situations)
	13. Appreciation (recognizing the relationship between the research process and lifelong learning; valuing information)

FINAL PRODUCTS

Now, students' I-Search papers should contain more than the answers to their research questions. They should demonstrate how the students select, evaluate, and use their information. The final products, or other written documents, should reveal how their thinking evolves as they read, collect, connect, and evaluate information to form their ideas. The writing should communicate their thoughts and feelings as they act upon each step of the research process. If the writing evidences these attributes, students will value information and feel confident in their abilities to use information to solve problems and make decisions throughout their lives. The I-Search is the vehicle to use, if there are effective strategies for implementing it. Macrorie's college composition class strategies do not transfer completely to K–12 students' needs.

The flow to the final steps and strategies is displayed in the chart in Figure 2.6.

> The I-Search narrative contains
> - What I Knew
> - Why I'm Writing This Paper
> - The Search
> - What I Learned

Figure 2.6.   Flowchart: Final Product Process Steps and Strategies

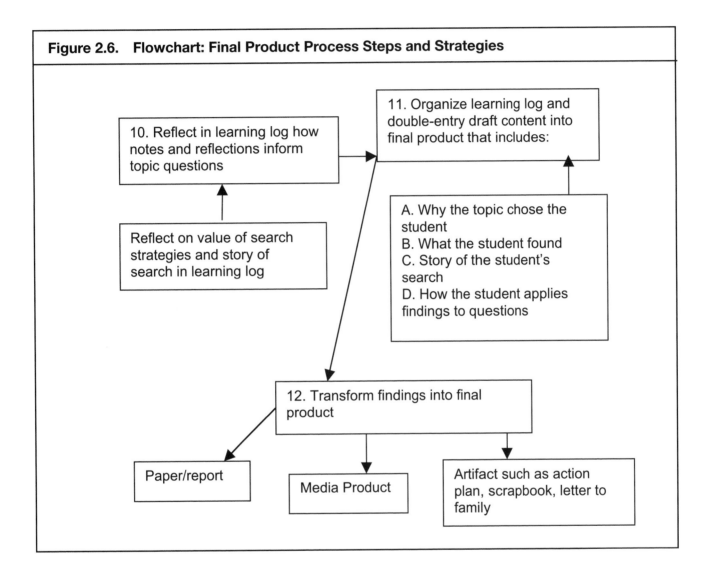

LOOKING AHEAD

It is time to move beyond Macrorie's methods and teach the I-Search as a research process to K–12 students. The following chapters explain the teaching methodologies and research strategies that make the I-Search an effective and productive research process. It takes time to develop expertise and good teaching relationships between classroom teachers and media specialists in implementing this process. Some now use it as a foundational research process before they assign more traditional research papers. Others use the I-Search as an investigatory process for younger students, but the I-Search is successful for all age groups in giving students a strong sense of effective research strategies. Defining the word *research* might still be difficult for some students, but they get a sense of what works and why it works. They use that sense to develop their research sophistication as they continue in school and in life. And that is what learning is all about.

REFERENCES

Kuhlthau, C. C. (1993). *Seeking meaning: A process approach to library information services.* Norwood, NJ: Ablex.

Macrorie, K. (1988). *The I-Search paper.* Rev. ed. Portsmouth, NH: Heinemann.

Maine Educational Media Association's Ad Hoc Committee on Information Skills. (1990). *Information skills guide for Maine educators.* Augusta, ME: Maine State Library.

Murray, D. M. (1982). "Writing as process: How writing finds its own meaning." In Murray, D. M. *Learning by teaching.* (pp. 17–31) Portsmouth, NH: Heinemann.

3 STARTING THE PROCESS

The I-Search method is a natural tool for collaboration among media specialists and teachers as well as a means for teaching research and writing. As teachers and media specialists working together, you share responsibilities for planning, teaching, and facilitating the unit. For example, collaboration between a content area teacher and a media specialist gives students two teachers for the I-Search unit, two facilitators, two idea people, more individualized attention, and, consequently, a stronger support system. Collaboration ensures that the I-Search unit contains writing, reading, and research process goals. Students see this team as teachers vested in their success and respond accordingly.

The key stages in the I-Search process are not only a formula for success but a method for teaching students successful research practices. They result from more than 30 collective years of experience in teaching the I-Search. Use the strategies separately or collectively, as needed, to design successful content units. Fit each unit with the strategies that contribute to content and information literacy objectives. The I-Search process lends itself to subject area investigations quite productively, giving students more ownership of their research. Use the I-Search to help students develop a research process foundation. In all uses, topic choice plays a critical role in building a solid set of personal research strategies.

THE ROLE OF FACILITATOR

The relationship between students and teachers is vital to the I-Search process, with the teacher and media specialist serving as facilitators. Students are collaborative partners in developing the process strategies through their input. When students are able to describe their frustrations and confusion, you can guide them through their obstacles. Facilitation means you work constantly with students to assess their progress. To meet the needs of students, you may need to modify plans, activities, and objectives when necessary.

If you follow curriculum standards, which are the models or examples that teachers should follow for each content area, even with a fairly prescribed curriculum, you will be surprised at how many of the standards one can cover in an I-Search content area unit. I-Search may, in fact, provide a sought-after opportunity to facilitate content learning through a creative research approach.

Students learn facts and conceptual understandings that stay with them and serve as building blocks for the future. Through their critical, reflective thinking, they learn to apply their new knowledge to their discipline studies, and make associations with their lives outside of the classroom. They learn how to create higher-order, authentic questions—questions that ask for more than factual knowledge (i.e., understandings, evaluative criteria, solutions, etc.) and relate to problems or aspects of the student's life. Grappling with higher-order, authentic questions forces students to think about what they are researching and how they are going to solve a problem or answer the question using their own ideas and information they have found.

Communication is a critical part of facilitation. To encourage student involvement in the content, engage them to think about the aspects of the content topic that interest them. Guide them to create questions that focus on what they are investigating and how they are learning. If they ask critical thinking questions about their topic, they have the opportunity to take responsibility for what they want to learn, which motivates them to learn for their own interest, not because the teacher requires it.

Facilitation means helping students discover how research strategies can work for them. It should help them make decisions about what the data shows as they research their topic questions, and help them evaluate and apply the data they find to their topic question. It does not mean assigning them a topic, giving them a deadline, and waiting until the papers cross the teacher's desk to critique their weaknesses.

> Communication is a critical part of facilitation.

PREPARE FOR THE UNIT

Included in this process are strategies and activities that have worked for a majority of students. Nevertheless, these strategies and activities are not ends in themselves. They facilitate the process as the student experiences it. If a strategy or technique does not meet the needs of an individual student or group of students, assist students in finding alternative strategies. Conferencing is the primary strategy for discovering students' needs.

Stay alert to students' problems by questioning your assumptions: about students, about what you teach, and about what your students need. Some of the best process teachers take this route. Atwell (1987) says, "I paved the way [for change] through reading and writing . . . through uncovering and questioning my as-

> Sharing the teacher's learning log with students involves them with the teaching/learning process.

sumptions, through observing kids and trying to make sense of my observations, through dumb mistakes, uncertain experiments, and underneath it all, the desire to do my best by my kids" (p. 4). Atwell gives herself permission to experiment with new methodologies and to make mistakes. Teachers who want students to develop good problem-solving strategies allow themselves to make mistakes modeling their own problem-solving. Providing acknowledged examples of weak strategizing can be as important as providing exemplars of good strategizing, if discussion follows.

Learning logs, which are journals containing the students' reflective thinking on strategies and information as it shapes their questions, are critical as a tool for developing and integrating I-Search strategies and progress assessment. A teacher's learning log containing reflections on students' use of strategies would give valuable insights into strategies that work and strategies that need adaptation or an alternative. Recording comments from conferences also serves as an effective method for monitoring students' progress. Moreover, reading student learning log entries uncovers new discoveries about strategies and connections that will strengthen the unit. Sharing your learning log entries with students helps students feel a part of the process. This involvement and interaction among students, the media specialist, and classroom teacher is a critical component of the I-Search unit.

OVERVIEW OF THE I-SEARCH PROCESS

The following overview of the strategies at the point of introduction into the I-Search process evolved from research and experiences in teaching the process. Although it does not show all points of iterations in the process, students frequently revisit steps, as needed. Note that use of the pre-notetaking sheet to create higher-order questions is a prime iteration point. A second draft of the pre-notetaking sheet, after students have read enough material to establish a knowledge base, is a tool for narrowing focus and creating higher-order questions that promote critical thinking. The outline in Figure 3.1 provides a synopsis of the critical events in the I-Search process.

Figure 3.1. Outline: The I-Search Process

I. Create personal universe web

    A. Choose interest area to explore

    B. Create interest topic web

II. Solicit questions and suggestions about interest areas from family, peers

    A. Participate in accordion strategy

    B. Share results

III. Create pre-notetaking sheet with three columns

    A. What I know

    B. What I don't know

    C. What I want to know through my research

IV. Read without notetaking from general sources to build background knowledge

    A. Do not take notes while reading in general sources

    B. Learn to skim and scan

    C. Wait until done with a session, then close source, reflect on how information informs topic in learning log

    D. Use teacher-created prompts to promote reflection

    E. Create bibliographic citations in proper form and keep them with notes in learning log

    F. Identify keywords and search terms

V. Create 2nd draft of pre-notetaking sheet

    A. Revise questions based on increased knowledge from general source reading

    B. Identify specific resources, including Internet websites, people to interview, media center holdings, etc.

VI. Use double-entry drafts for reflective notetaking from resources

    A. For each resource, write bibliographic citation on double-entry draft page

    B. Take notes from sources in left column on double-entry draft page

    C. Reflect on notes in right column on double-entry draft page

    D. Use teacher prompts for reflections, if desired

VII. Apply the findings to the research question

VIII. Reflect on value of search strategies in learning log

    IX. Organize learning log reflections, double-entry draft entries, and reflections into final product (format can be student's choice) which includes:

    A. Why the topic chose the student

    B. Story of the student's search

    C. What the student found

    D. How the student answered the question or solved the problem

FOUR KEYS TO I-SEARCH

The four key sections of the I-Search process are:

- choose a topic,
- find information,
- use the right information, and
- present the result in a format that makes the most sense for the topic.

This last step could be a paper, a journal, an action plan, a Microsoft PowerPoint presentation, an Inspiration diagram, or an image such as a photograph album, poster, or design drawing. It can be presented online or orally. Each key section has a number of strategies for facilitating this stage of the process. Some of the strategies recur throughout the I-Search. A typical example is the practice of reflective reading, which consists of reflecting on the information you have read to make sense of it in terms of the question you want to answer. Students first engage in reflective reading after they have drawn up their initial ideas on what they know about a topic, what they don't know, and what they want to know (pre-notetaking strategy). A good strategy is for teachers and media specialists to guide students to background information; then ask, them not to take notes, but to think about how the information they find relates to and informs their topic.

Then students take time immediately after reading each general resource to note the bibliographic citation in their learning logs and reflect on how what they have learned changes their knowledge of their topic and what they might want to investigate—i.e., their "what I want to know" questions.

Students often find reading without immediate notetaking a difficult strategy to use. With practice and encouragement, they engage their minds more deeply with their reading content and focus on their questions. They manage to skip the information that previously gained their attention but had no bearing on their questions. The lack of notetaking while students read the general source materials ensures that students do not get bogged down in trivia about the topic or get waylaid by interesting but nonessential facts. If students translate their topics into interesting questions that facilitate a good research experience, copying and pasting does not tempt them as much.

> Reading general resource material without notetaking is a difficult but important strategy for strengthening background knowledge.

PREPARE STUDENTS FOR METACOGNITIVE THINKING

The I-Search process is different from many classroom assignments because it requires students to think metacognitively—they must "think about their thinking." To introduce students to this concept, ask each student to keep a learning log in which they record their actions, thoughts, and feelings as they move through the I-Search unit. The log provides access to their thoughts as they react to the information they collect and attempt to apply it to their problem. The learning log also serves as a place for them to record and reflect on the success of their search and the strategies they use. When they put together their final product, they will refer back to the learning log for much of their narrative. Depending on the requirements for the unit, the final version or product might even be an edited version of the learning log, reorganized into the four main sections of the I-Search final product.

REFLECT ON PRIOR RESEARCH EXPERIENCES

If students reflect on their prior research experiences for a first activity in the I-Search unit, it will set the stage for a more productive appreciation of the new research process experience. When students comment about past research assignments, they start to think reflectively and critically about the strategies they used. The following prompts will help them respond verbally or in their learning logs:

1. What are some of the research projects you have done?
2. From these projects, what does *research* mean to you?
3. Describe one of your research successes. Why was the experience positive?
4. Describe one of your research failures. Why was the experience negative?

Students' responses will probably reveal a frustration with traditional research methods. Very few students recall more than a single, successful research project, or one with a connection to their lives. More telling, they probably cannot adequately describe

Very few students retain memories of successful K–12 research projects.

a good research process. It is clearly evident that very few students feel that their previous school research experiences have been valuable. Consequently, they rarely use any of the traditional research strategies to answer questions outside of school. They do not carry over their school research process to use as adults when they have crucial issues to explore, such as buying a new car, having children, or discovering the effects of various medical treatments for a friend or family member.

Thus, to embed the research process strategies and make them useful beyond the present school assignment, it is extremely important to encourage students to relate the research/writing experience to what happens in their lives. This is reasonably easy if teachers have time to help students experience a full I-Search with choice of a personal topic, but harder if the need is to develop essential content area questions that pique their interest. The key is to find topics—from science to social studies to literature—that have a connection with their lives outside of school.

The most pressing barriers that seem to deter teachers from using the I-Search research/writing process within their curricula seem to be whether the I-Search would work with a content area topic and the time it would take to include an I-Search unit. One of the reasons for these barriers is that many teachers do not think in terms of having students create their questions about a topic. Given an assigned topic, if the student brainstorms about the topic and has a chance to choose an interest area and develop a higher-order question concerning it, the student will still have motivation to perform at a higher level than previously. Separating a topic into parts that are researchable, brainstorming possibilities, choosing one of those possibilities, and developing higher-order questions (how, why, which, etc.) all stimulate student interest in content area topics. With this approach, much of the power of the I-Search integrates into the research unit. The remaining strategies fit naturally within the research activities and do not increase the time frame necessary for the research. One caveat is that teachers will need to scaffold the creation of higher-order questions, because of students' lack of practice.

Herein is the difference with many research assignments. In a traditional research scenario, teachers assign topics, not topic questions, for which students collect and summarize information and ideas that they write about in a third-person format. The I-Search strategies, on the other hand, motivate students to use information to solve problems, answer questions they've asked, and/or make decisions. This process approach greatly increases student learning growth in a content area research assignment. Solving problems, answering higher-order questions that require critical

> Relating the topic to students' lives creates motivation and interest.

> Solving problems, answering higher-order questions that require critical thinking about gathered information, and making decisions about content issues are primary strategies for getting students connected to their content topic.

thinking about the gathered information, and making decisions about content issues are primary strategies for getting students connected to their content topic. These activities dramatically decrease the copy-paste-regurgitation paper.

By requiring the critical strategies, such as brainstorming content area topics and creating questions, teachers facilitate students' conceptual understanding of research. Effective research helps students build a new perspective about a concept, discover new ideas, and gather information to make a decision and to suggest a variety of solutions to a problem. Students have had the idea that research is straight reportage of facts for so long, that their research habits are ingrained and more difficult to change. This book suggests the I-Search works best when students have total topic choice, but using the I-Search strategies, singly or collectively, when students have to stay within an assigned content area, can be equally successful. Each strategy helps them improve the success of their research process, learning, and product.

Sharing research successes and nightmares from students' personal experiences will help teachers and media specialists explain many of the objectives for an I-Search. For example, students' comments on topic selection frequently reflect the importance of picking personally meaningful topics. One of our students noted: "A positive research assignment that stands out in my mind was an autobiography that I did last year. It gave me a chance to find out about my past and relatives. . . . I found out things about myself that I never knew before." Another student enjoyed his science fair project on the behavior of fish because it made him a better fisherman. A third student found his math project on Pascal's triangle "long and boring" until he was able to relate his information to what he was learning in a computer programming class. Such responses are a natural introduction to "the topic choosing you."

Research nightmares are also a tool for previewing the obstacles that students encounter during the process. "I couldn't come up with a topic." "I didn't know how to start." "It was hard to put [the information] in my own words." "My science teacher made us collect leaves and identify them. We all had to scramble down to the library before all three of the books on leaves were taken out." "I always wait until the night before to do it. Then my parents get mad because I stay up all night." "I had lots of stuff on notecards. But I couldn't figure out how to organize them!"

Such student comments help other students understand the obstacles that they will face, as well as the purpose of the learning log and types of assessment. All researchers encounter obstacles. The goal is to find strategies and techniques for overcoming them. Their learning logs are excellent places for discussing their problems and describing possible solutions. Students evaluate and reflect on the actions they take to solve the problems. When teachers and media specialists read the learning logs, they can make suggestions that support the students, guide them, and facilitate a solution.

Give students credit for keeping a log of their activities and make sure they reflect on their failures as well as successes. The enticement of credit usually encourages hesitant students to try to reflect. Most students are impressed that you care about their thoughts and feelings. They also like the idea that they have individual assistance throughout the project. Sharing their thoughts and the promise of individual assistance, made possible because of the collaboration between the teacher and media specialist, establish a positive atmosphere for the unit. Sharing of learning logs is also one of the most effective ways to conference with students. What they write will provide clues for the support they need.

CHOOSE A TOPIC

Choosing a topic "that itches" might be simple for adults who bring many life experiences to an I-Search and face many problems both big and small in their daily lives. But what will students do who have fewer life experiences and little practice in acknowledging them? Some students will draw a blank when asked to choose a topic.

If the class brainstorms topics together for an I-Search when the topics are to be within a content area, students start to think about what interests them. Reading articles in journals, books, or newspapers; searching the Internet after learning how to evaluate Web sites; and interviewing family or local experts give students opportunities to boost their basic knowledge about the content area and identify specific resources for further investigation. Introducing background knowledge in the content area before the I-Search assignment is a necessity, to provide students with enough information to brainstorm interesting topics.

When the topic is their choice entirely, a personal universe web graphically illustrates students' lives, including interests, hobbies, family, friends, and school. One area to discourage, if possible, is attention to "hot topics," such as rock groups, celebrities in the news, or current trends. These topics usually bore students once

A personal universe web graphically illustrates the important aspects of a student's life.

they start their investigations, while topics related to their own life experiences stimulate enthusiasm and interest. Teachers and media specialists scaffold the webbing activity by interviewing each other about their own life interests, with one person drawing a web on the smart board and filling in the other's answers to interview questions. Students see through the example how to create a good web that will give them more than one topic possibility. Students enjoy watching the adults go through the process.

SEARCH THE WEB

Web milestones should relate to an experience, an event, a person, a significant item, or a place.

After modeling the creation of a personal universe web, have students create their own personal universe webs, consisting of several major milestones in their lives, in their learning logs. These milestones should relate to an experience, an event, a person, a significant item, or a place. The universe web depicted in Figure 3.2 is an example of how students can identify experiences graphically.

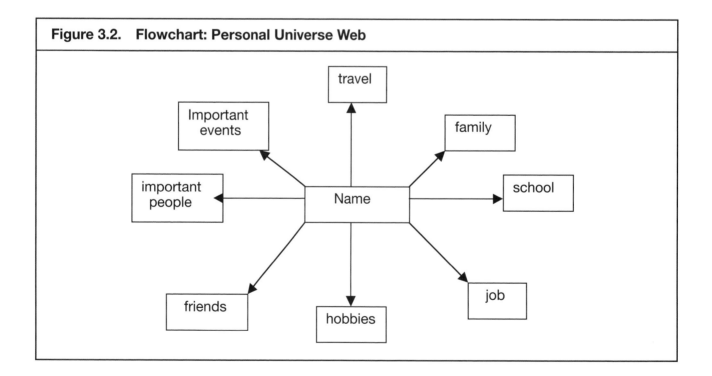

Figure 3.2. Flowchart: Personal Universe Web

To support students in creating their personal universe web, provide the following instructions:

- For each major balloon on the web, list a milestone in your life. Leave space around each of these milestone balloons so that you will be able to surround each of them with other connecting balloons.
- Around each milestone, make balloons listing the first two or three connections that pop into your head, such as people, places, or incidents related to the milestone.
- Around that first layer of connected balloons, create a second layer for each balloon consisting of experiences concerning the milestone.
- Fill a third layer of balloons around each balloon in the second layer with how the milestone is significant. How did it affect you? What did it show about your strengths or weaknesses, plans for the future, career choices, and/ or personal goals?

The student's goal is to obtain as many details about the milestones as possible. Students find a partner and use questions to help each other identify interest areas. Here is an example:

Questioner: What is an important event in your life?

Subject: My parents just told me that we would be moving.

Questioner: Tell me about moving.

Subject: We will be moving to Seattle, Washington, in the middle of the school year. I have to leave my friends and the baseball team. I won't know anyone there. I don't know if I will be able to play on the baseball team. I worry that I won't be good enough to play.

Questioner: Why do you think you won't be able to play?

Subject: It will be a much bigger school. The league will be tougher. There will be many more boys trying out.

Tell students to find relationships between items on each other's web. Which items on the web arouse their curiosity and require more information? What else do they want to know about the participant? After generating as many responses as possible for each balloon added to the web, the student looks for repeated ideas or themes that can lead to an I-Search. One participant talks about her love of animals. She describes her fondness for cats and enjoyment of wild animals. Her partner helps her discover a possible I-Search topic related to animal rights.

Demonstrating web diagramming takes about 40 minutes. Involving other adults in the process, especially those close to the student, is particularly helpful. Frequently, students fail to recognize the important events and people in their lives. In spite of his web, one student thought about searching one of those "hot topics," UFOs, until he spoke to his parents: "They really didn't like any of my topics but gave me two topics they were curious about. First, my father told me that he was curious about Ireland because his ancestors came from Ireland. . . . Next I talked to my mother. She told me that she had been curious about my cousin Kristy, who has autism. I liked this topic quite a bit because I was curious about why she acts the way she does." Exploring the topic of autism added a bonus of guaranteed parental interest in the final result.

LEARNING LOGS

The reflective process begins at the beginning of the topic search with the learning log as a tool. The logs serve as both a journal of reflective thoughts and a place to create and reflect on the products they create, such as the personal universe web and the double-entry drafts. The flowchart in Figure 3.3 illustrates the process of information entry into the learning log and the kinds of reflective possibilities.

Figure 3.3.   Learning Log Flowchart

Introduction
- Why I chose my topic
- What I already know about my topic
- Questions I want to answer through my search

If I changed my topic, add
- The description of the original topic
- The reason for the change

Pre-notetaking and Background Reading
- What I learned about content and process from my pre-notetaking and background reading, listening, viewing, and interviewing
- How my topic and research questions evolved as a result of my initial explorations

My reactions to I-Search strategies (e.g., brainstorming, peer conferencing, the pre-notetaking process)

Interaction With Resources*
- To what degree the resource helped answer research questions
- New insights and learning
- Changes in thinking as a result of new learning
- Evaluation of quality of resource
- Comparison/contrast of resource with other resources for content and quality
- Next step

Add relevant personal reactions to the process:
- Frustrations
- Obstacles encountered and potential solutions
- Explanation of why the solutions succeeded or failed
- Observations on process tools (e.g., double-entry drafts and learning logs) and their effectiveness
- Reflections on personal learning style
- Reflections on peer conferences and interaction with instructor (e.g., questions and responses)

Conclusion
- What I learned about my topic
- What I learned about research strategies and techniques
- What I learned about the process of information seeking and how I will apply it to my work as a librarian

If my search is incomplete at the time of the due date
- Whether or not the search will continue
- Any future plans

***Note:** Your writing for this section should be based on the content and responses from your double-entry draft for each resource. Select the items that relate to the evolution of the I-Search. Include information on both content and process. <u>Remember, you are telling the story of your journey.</u>

Personal universe webs should be the first document entered into the learning log. Reflection on the web comes next. Students need plenty of time to reflect on their choice of topic and write about their thoughts on the topic in their logs. Sometimes this reflective period results in a powerful choice, such as Beth's topic:

> I was walking through the house looking at old pictures when I saw a picture of my Gramma Shirley (my Dad's mother). I asked my mom what she died of, and that's how I came up with ALS (Amyotrophic Lateral Sclerosis). From that point on, I was curious about what the disease does to you, how it develops, the first symptoms, and whether or not it's hereditary. The idea of ALS being hereditary played a huge role in my decision of this topic. I was really scared about whether I was going to die in my late forties. Why be scared!? Another major factor was I wanted to find out about the disease that killed my grandmother, whether she suffered and what she went through. I don't think I will ever stop searching for facts until they find a cure and know what causes it.

Because reflection time is so important in the I-Search pre-search process, if teachers begin the I-Search before a vacation, it works well. Students complete the webbing exercise just prior to the vacation and then use the time to discuss the various topics that interest them with their parents and others. Students can speak with family members and relatives about family history and important events.

When they return, students use their webs to isolate two or three possible topics and record their thoughts and feelings about their topics in their learning logs. Writing prompts help them record how their topic chooses them. If they still have several choices that draw them, they should prioritize with reasons or reflect on pros and cons. This is also the time to have them reflect on the value of the webbing strategy as a scaffold for choosing a topic.

Next, they create a topic web around their chosen topic. This web helps them sort out what they know and what they don't know, which can be difficult for many people. This web also belongs in the learning log and provides clues into the kinds of resources the student will require. Your flexibility through these steps aids students who do not do well with graphics as learning tools. For them, outlining is an alternative to the web. The drawing software now available has excellent capabilities for creating both outlines and webs. Its use should be encouraged because of

---

Writing prompts help students reflect on their topic choice progress.

its flexibility in format and ability to help the student think while creating the graphics and/or outline.

Sometimes students change their topics after reflection and webbing. Some students come back from their reflection period with an entirely different topic as a result of conversations. Other students find a topic of immediate importance in their lives and do not have to go through a decision-making step. Students who choose potentially controversial topics or private topics require a teacher conference with parents and the student to ensure that parents support the choice, or a variation of the topic. An example of this type of topic would be an exploration of one's adoption to discover one's birth parents. In this case, the teacher, parents, and student settled on encouraging the student to explore the process for finding birth parents, but not the actual search.

A recounting of what the student already knows about the topic goes next into the learning log. This information will prove valuable when the student settles on research questions through the following pre-notetaking strategy.

WRITING PROMPTS

As a further strategy, the following "sentence starters" help students reflect on their progress in choosing a topic. Students expand the sentence starters into a paragraph with their thoughts and opinions on the strategies, such as webbing, or diagram software programs.

1. I learned the following information about myself through my web:
2. I think webbing helped/did not help me find a topic because:
3. I want to consider the following two or three topics for my I-Search:
4. My first choice of a topic is ———— because:
5. I know the following about my first choice:

If possible, students have time to write in class with the media specialist and teacher present to facilitate the process. At this stage facilitation includes:

- working with individual students to draw out subjects that should be included in the learning log;
- asking questions to help students generate details; and
- having students with good learning log entries read their responses to the class, thus providing others with good models.

DEBRIEF SESSIONS

The end of the writing period in class is a good time for debriefing student thoughts on the process with the class. Where are they in the process of topic choice? What strategies are working for them—e.g., the personal web, the outline? What problems are they encountering and how can they overcome them? What is their next step? If a student says that he/she is frustrated by a lack of information in the personal web, is the student talking with peers, parents, teachers, or the media specialist? By discussing successes as well as frustrations or confusions, students can identify problems and work as a group to solve them. The debriefing time also establishes an atmosphere of collaboration among the media specialist, teacher, and students. This process is especially important in large classes in which individual help is less available.

> Debriefing establishes an atmosphere of class collaboration.

SKIM AND SCAN RESOURCES

Students are now ready to use media center resources for the initial exploration of their topics, in order of preference. For students whose topics have chosen them, skimming and scanning material about their subjects in general encyclopedias and in specialized reference materials, browsing abstracts and articles on electronic databases, and skimming relevant Web sites and chapters of books start what might be called a "feeding frenzy." The more they learn, the more they want to know. This initial investigation of potential sources is also an opportunity to insert any missing information-finding skills.

CONFERENCES

Recognizing the need for individual conferencing and knowing when to intervene are key components of the process approach to teaching research. Kuhlthau (1993) interprets intervention as "mediation into areas where individuals cannot proceed on their own, or can advance only with great difficulty" (p.155). Conferencing with individual students, debriefing students at the beginning or end of a class, and reading learning logs are strategies that help determine when to intervene.

The initial exploration of potential topics usually involves two days of working in the media center, with time for students to share their topics with the class and explain how the "topics chose them." Students sit in a circle and share their topics with the entire class. If time is limited or the class is large, the class splits into groups of four or five with students sharing their topics within their groups. Student interaction with their peers at this phase of the I-Search process serves several purposes. The need to find the words to communicate their topics and goals forces students to articulate their thoughts. Input from classmates, usually in the form of questions, helps students clarify vague language, identify a related idea worth exploring, and hear about a good source of information. A positive response from peers validates a student's work and choice, increasing the level of comfort.

The next chapter includes more of the pre-search process, introducing the use of a pre-notetaking sheet for narrowing the topic focus, resource searching, and background reading.

> Conferencing and recognizing when to intervene are key components of the process approach.

REFERENCES

Atwell, N. (1987). *In the middle*. Portsmouth, NH: Heinemann.

Kuhlthau, C. C. (1993). *Seeking meaning: A process approach to library information services*. Norwood, NJ: Ablex.

4 NARROWING THE TOPIC

After students make their topic choice, it's time to move them to the second phase of the I-Search. This part of the research process has three tasks:

- narrow the topic,
- find a focus, and
- create the research questions.

These tasks help students who have a topic, their thesis statements, and tentative outlines, but do not know how to transfer thesis statements to questions. The strategies in this chapter support student efforts to put their topics into higher-order researchable questions. They also support a type of notetaking that encourages immediate reflection on the information the student wishes to save from the resource.

Thesis statements do not ensure that students know how to define what they need to investigate in their research. The I-Search strategies provide effective scaffolding which supports student attempts to create higher-order researchable questions before they start collecting resources or taking notes on their topic. If students start taking notes immediately with only the thesis statement as a basis for their research, they probably will collect too much useless, but interesting, information. Strong scaffolding for building good researchable questions helps students narrow the kinds of information they should gather. A research question helps them focus their information search on what they can use to develop their own perspectives on the topic, to investigate and suggest one or more solutions to the posed problem, or to brainstorm ideas about their topics. This pre-search stage is essential to successful research but is frequently missing for many students, and not emphasized by their teachers. The students skip right by it.

Students commonly start collecting resources and taking notes before they have sufficiently settled on questions that fit their topic or thesis statement. What do they do with these bits of information? Usually, they put them on notecards and then try to organize their notes in some fashion, such as chronological, and present it for the teacher's enlightenment. Unfortunately, many of them have not evaluated and synthesized their information. Their papers contain a series of cut-and-paste information blurbs, sometimes with good transitions, many times not. When students do not have a focus for their research, they do not have a perspective on what information is important to their topic or how it informs their topic. Thus, many students pad their papers with

> The second phase of the I-Search process consists of:
> - narrowing the topic,
> - finding the focus, and
> - creating the research questions.

everything they find to meet the paper's required length. When teachers focus on the paper's structure—i.e., whether the paper fits the pre-set requirements for form, grammatical correctness, length, and number of resources, they often slight their evaluation of the student's content synthesis. When this happens, the student could receive an A grade for minimal thinking about a topic.

One answer to this research conundrum appears in a research process model (Maine Educational Media Association's Ad Hoc Committee on Information Skills, 1990) adopted in Maine, which has four components in its structure, the first of which (pre-search) contains the following steps:

Step 1. Students form a tentative, essential research question, which is one of the most difficult steps in the process. Creating an essential question, which requires the student to analyze, evaluate, and synthesize information through higher-order conceptual thinking, is a skill that most students do not possess. Consequently, they do not attempt to create questions to focus their research and instead, concentrate, on finding factual information easily borrowed and pasted into a paper in whatever order makes sense to them.

When students develop higher-order essential questions about their topic, they create a structure and focus for their research. This emphasis demands and facilitates higher-order thinking, which increases their ability to generate fresh perspectives about their topic and integrate their learning into their long-term memory.

Step 2. Students connect questions to prior knowledge. Many students will have little or no foundation knowledge, even about topics that are interesting to them. Thus, if they participate in a "reading without notetaking" strategy, it will help them build an understanding about the topic area without bogging them down with constant notetaking. They can focus on reading for topic background information, while thinking about their proposed questions. For most students, this is a very hard task; they easily revert to writing down most of what they read, even from generalized resources that give them broad conceptual understandings, not details.

Step 3. Students identify key words and names involved with their topic. This skill depends on their background knowledge of the research content area.

Step 4. Students develop essential questions into questions that focus and structure the search. Few students know how to write higher-order researchable questions without scaffolding. It is a skill that requires practice. Possibly because the skill is time-consum-

---

Pre-search steps
- **Step 1:** Create a tentative research question(s)
- **Step 2:** Connect the question to prior knowledge
- **Step 3:** Identify key words and search terms
- **Step 4:** Develop questions that focus and structure the search
- **Step 5:** Make adjustments to the essential question and its focus

---

Use these prompts to help students respond to general reading without notetaking in their learning logs.
- What new discoveries did they make?
- How are these discoveries influencing their thinking?
- What new connections are they making as a result of collecting new information?
- Do they need to modify their action plan in light of new information?

ing and difficult to master, many teachers choose to forgo question-making and, instead, assign theme paper topics that do not require transitioning the topics to essential questions. Given such topics, students rush to locate all the information they can gather about the topic and then "dump" it into final products. Without scaffolding and reflection, students do not process information into new perspectives about their topic.

Step 5. Students make adjustments to the essential research question and its focus. This step can continue up to the preliminary draft, as students begin to understand how they will answer the research question. Frequently, new understandings motivate the student to change the research focus to include new ideas and perspectives about the topic.

Finding the eventual focus is an evolutionary process that reflects Murray's (1980) model of writing as information processing. Question-making is quite difficult for most students accustomed to being handed a topic. The first strategy is to have students brainstorm all parts of the topic, relying on their prior knowledge. As students recall prior knowledge, they create webs that show the relationship of these knowledge bits to each other.

The I-Search includes a strategy called the "accordion exercise" to use at this point in the research project. The accordion exercise is very popular with students. Most students like to know what their peers consider a good question about their topic. The activity starts when all students think they have at least a tentative topic. They fold an $8\frac{1}{2} \times 11$ sheet of paper horizontally in small folds, until it resembles a hand-held fan (see Figure 4.1).

> The accordion exercise is a popular way to enlist peer support in creating topic questions.

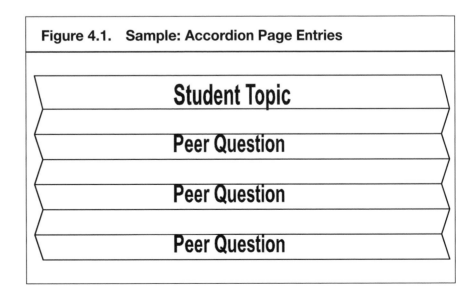

Figure 4.1. Sample: Accordion Page Entries

Student Topic

Peer Question

Peer Question

Peer Question

At the top of the sheet they write their topic, which should not be stated as a question. A good prompt for them might be, "I want to know about . . . " When they finish folding their papers, they pass their own paper to the person on the left (or right). If the group is large, they split up into smaller groups or pass the topics within the row to consume less class time. When the person on their left gets a new sheet with a topic, they think of something that they, too, would like to know about the topic. They try to write it as a question on one of the spaces between folds in the paper, taking care not to look at anyone else's questions, which could influence them. Students pass along these papers and comment on topics until their own arrives back to them. Most of the time, they express surprise at the breadth of questions. The accordion exercise gives them a number of queries about their topic that they could consider developing as an essential question in the *how, why,* or *which* format. Then, as students reflect on these new questions, they start filling in the pre-notetaking sheet, a strategy that scaffolds creating interesting higher-order questions.

> Conferencing scaffolds students' ability to create higher order questions.

PRE-NOTETAKING STRATEGY

Rankin (1988) describes an effective strategy for finding a focus, which builds into an idea for the I-Search pre-notetaking strategy. Call (1991) has a similar model, the *What I know* sheet. Rankin and her teaching partner have their middle school students list what they know about their subjects and then add what they do not know. The *What I Don't Know* section makes this strategy different from the commonly used KWL format, *Know, Want to Know, Learned.* The pre-notetaking sheet utilizes *What I Don't Know* instead of *Learned,* which assumes students will return to the KWL sheet at the end of their research. Instead of returning to the *Learned* column, the pre-notetaking sheet includes as the third and last column, *What I Want to Know.* This places the pre-notetaking drafts totally in the pre-search stage of the research process. Reflecting by students on what they don't know stimulates interest and curiosity. What students record in the *What I Don't Know* column forms the basis for creating their essential and related questions in the *What I Know* column.

> Students use the pre-notetaking strategy to record:
> - *What I Know*
> - *What I Don't Know*
> - *What I Want to Know*

Figure 4.2. Template: Pre-Notetaking Sheet

What I Know about My Topic	What I Don't Know about My Topic	What I Want to Know about My Topic
		[These questions should lead to your essential question(s).]

Use *how, why,* and *which* question starters with key words to create higher-order questions. Higher-order research questions promote critical thinking

- *How* questions discover a process.
- *Why* questions seek an explanation.
- *Which* questions compare and contrast two or more ideas or concepts.

Students use their peers' most interesting questions from the accordion activity to record possibilities in the *What I Don't Know* column. They also contribute their own *What I Don't Know* thoughts after reflecting on their *What I Know* information from their prior experiences and prior knowledge. Sometimes students find this a difficult list to create. Have them generate another web or outline exclusively on their topic choice, using what they know and what others have suggested through the accordion activity. Visualizing their topic and its related parts in the web or outline structure gives an extra opportunity for stimulating what they don't know and might want to know.

Finally, the third column, *What I Want to Know,* is a place to record several related questions that interest them from the *What I Don't Know* column. They work these questions into a higher-order essential question that they want to investigate. At this point, teacher/media specialist conferencing with the student is usually necessary to scaffold the question-making. Many times, the questions at this stage begin with word prompts, such as *what, when, does,* and *is,* that ask for factual answers and yes/no decisions. Have them categorize their questions and then create investigative questions starting with higher-order prompts, such as *how, why,* or *which* or other action verbs that demand original thinking.

If their questions stay at the knowledge level on Bloom's *Taxonomy of Educational Objectives* (1974), they usually produce a report that typically does not involve their own ideas and reflective thinking. Knowledge level questions make it easy for them to slip back into the habitual reporting of facts about a topic, with little or no metacognitive analysis.

The I-Search objective is to have students experience much more power within a research experience than a reporting of information. The I-Search integrates an investigative process that transfers to multiple situations, but only if students create questions that challenge them to think. Higher-order questions help them discover a process (*How . . .*), seek an explanation (*Why . . .*), or compare and contrast two or more ideas or concepts (*Which . . .*).

The art of questioning, however, is a skill that most students do not practice once out of primary school, although they practice it constantly in their daily lives: "*Why* does this item cost so much?" "*Which* movie shall we see?" "*Why* are my parents so restrictive?" "*How* can I pay for a new car?" "*How* can I get a date for the dance Friday night?"

When the teacher and the media specialist slip back into roles as knowledge experts, they eliminate the need for students to discover and create understandings about the content areas they are studying. Students revert to listening to what the knowledge experts have to say and give it back on a test. Thus, they get very little practice in making the leap from creating and answering a factual question to creating and investigating a higher-order concept question that poses a problem or asks for a process, an explanation, or a comparison. The difference in these latter questions from a factual question is one of the central reasons why the I-Search process uses the pre-notetaking sheet to scaffold students' question-making. It supports their move away from yes/no questions that encourage copy-and-paste research, into questions that require critical thinking. The first draft of the pre-notetaking sheet will, in fact, be the start of an iterative process that produces the final essential question(s) and its subquestions.

BACKGROUND READING

After students finish the first draft of questions in the *What I Want to Know* column on the pre-notetaking sheet, and they've categorized and rewritten their questions into higher-order questions, introduce them to the strategy of general reading for topic background information.

Show students how to read general information resources by skimming and scanning without notetaking.

When they finish with each different resource, have them close the resource, write the bibliographic citation into their learning logs, and reflect about what they learned in general about their topic. They also note whether or not they need to refer again to

> General reading without notetaking helps students focus on background knowledge about their topics.

> Skimming and scanning are excellent reading process skills.

this resource, possibly for additional bibliography or facts they want to retain. Have them use this method for several general information resources to expand their general knowledge about their topic and decide whether their current version of their questions is what they want to know. This is not the time for them to read a specific and detailed resource to answer their questions. Get them thinking more in terms of skimming electronic or print encyclopedias or general reference materials. This strategy takes adjustment on their part, to break the common habit of taking notes immediately on everything they read. It keeps them focusing more on their topic in general than on specific facts.

Reading without notetaking helps students who do not have an adequate prior knowledge of their topic or are having difficulty creating questions that go beyond factual answers. For example, the student who wants to investigate a favorite relative's illness probably has limited knowledge but a strong personal interest. General reading will help him/her fill in the information gaps and construct strong research questions. It also will help the student discover the breadth of the topic and whether the focus should be narrowed. The student will learn the basic vocabulary and discover a direction to take in creating questions.

Other students might want to change their topics when they find that they cannot understand what they are reading. Conferences with these students might reveal that they need a better introduction to the specialized vocabulary associated with their topic. Other students might claim that they cannot read the material they find on their topic. Perhaps they are trying to read the most difficult article first, instead of beginning with articles from a general perspective.

THE PROCESS OF READING WITHOUT NOTETAKING

Students might need several class periods to finish their general reading. The need for starting with general sources is often a difficult concept for students to grasp. They want to jump into their research immediately. At the end of each class period, students need some time for learning log reflection. This helps stem the desire to take notes while reading that comes from the student's need to seek details that could go into the paper, even before they discover what they need to know.

To aid students' ability to reflect on and write about their general reading, ask students to address the following questions in their learning logs:

- What new discoveries did you make?
- How did you react to what you read?
- How could you use that information to help you solve your problem or answer your question?
- What other pieces of information do you remember and how could you apply them?
- What other questions emerge as a result of new information?

Writing reactions to these questions from their reading should help students create ownership of how they put their information findings together to answer their questions. What they write in their learning log from their background reading is in their own words because the resource is closed. Do not forget to have them keep track of their bibliographic citations associated with their reflections.

Background reading without notetaking helps students focus on the relationship of the information they are reading to their proposed essential question. This is a strategy for getting students to think about what they read in terms of their questions, instead of blindly copying down everything that interests them. This strategy also encourages the students' personal response to the topic. By easing the burden of sorting through many isolated pieces of information, students gain a frame of reference for dealing with information sources. They learn the common viewpoints associated with their subjects. They find points of comparison and contrast. By reflecting in their learning logs, they develop a platform to test out the information against their feelings and prior knowledge.

After students utilize these general resources effectively without notetaking, introduce them to the use of key words and Internet search engines and available electronic databases. Give them articles from newspapers and magazines so they can practice skimming and scanning until they get comfortable with the idea that they don't need minute details at this point. Make this a class exercise to pool everyone's ideas of what is important in the article and what key words to remember. Once they have discovered key ideas about the topic, have them transfer these ideas into key words to use in a potential research question. Practice is usually necessary, especially for older students who have a deeply ingrained habit of getting out the notecards or highlighter immediately when assigned a research topic.

At this stage of the process, students also start to develop their working bibliography by keeping track of these general resources and any additional sources they discover. This is the time to give them the citation format to use. Even though the I-Search provides the opportunity for a variety of final products, a bibliography and proper crediting of sources are essential. The back of the pre-notetaking sheet is a good space for students to list their sources in the proper format. Give them examples of citations for interviews, Web sites, books, and journal articles. As students start their reading, show them how to look for other resources in the bibliographies attached to their reading. When they find conflicting information, teach them how to compare and contrast the information and check with additional sources for validity and reliability. When the information they find leads to a new idea or conflicts with their previous assumptions or findings, have them evaluate their information or refine their questions, thus taking on the true role of a researcher.

Figure 4.3.   Template: Bibliography Sheet

Bibliography Sheet

This sheet is available for you to start listing the resources you think you will want to use for your research. Note the following information for each type of source so you have it when you complete your project's bibliography, using the style your teacher requests.

Note the following information for each book or article you want to use.

1. Author of book or article:
2. Title of book or article:
3. Date of publication for book or article:
4. Place of publication if book:
5. Publisher if book:
6. Journal title if article:
7. Volume number and issue number if journal article:
8. Page numbers for article in journal:

Note the following information for each Web site you want to use.
1. Author if available:
2. Title of Web page:
3. Date Web page was created:
4. Retrieved month day, year, from source URL:

Note the following information for each knowledge expert (include parent, friend, local expert, national expert, teacher, community member) you want to interview.
1. Name of interviewee:
2. Name of interviewer (if you did not do the interviewing):
3. Date of interview:
4. Type of interview (face-to-face; telephone; fax; e-mail; synchronous interactive voice):
5. Title or professional background of interviewee if relevant:

Source 1:

Source 2:

Source 3:

QUESTION-MAKING

Question-making is an important area where the I-Search is iterative. Returning to the essential question to check if it is still valid is not only possible, but expected, throughout the I-Search experience. When students complete their general reading without notetaking and before they start with their detailed reading, have them evaluate and revise their research questions, if necessary, using a second pre-notetaking sheet draft.

Before they prepare a second draft, model how to move their questions to a higher level on Bloom's *Taxonomy*. Ask students to create a list of key words from their readings. Then, have them combine each key word with one or more of the question starters *how, why,* and *which* to create a question about the topic. Have them record their questions on a new copy of their pre-notetaking sheet. To support students who want to go beyond creating questions with *who, what, when,* and *where,* ask them to think in terms of how something happened, why it happened, and how comparing and contrasting, or tracing a change over a period of time, predicting, and classifying could help them answer what they need to know. Give them a list of action verbs based on Bloom's *Taxonomy* to jump-start their thinking about their questions.

After generating as many questions as possible for *What I Want to Know,* ask students to choose several related questions that could serve as a focus for research on this topic, then have them choose the one question that overarches most of the others. This question should serve as their essential question. Model how to move beyond questions that ask only for facts to questions that require evaluation, analysis, and synthesis of the information they find is important. Figure 4.4 provides a handout summarizing how to create research questions, which should support the students' efforts.

> A second pre-notetaking draft is useful for revising and refining research questions.

Figure 4.4. Handout: How to Write Research Questions

How to Write Research Questions

1. Use the key words and names you have written on your personal web, received from your peers in the accordion exercise, or discovered during your general background reading to create questions to guide your research.

2. Questions that start with *how, why,* and *which* will most likely be your essential questions that focus your research.

    How questions search for a process or action, i.e., "How do I decide upon the right car to buy?" You would respond by deciding upon and indicating the steps you will take to make your car decision.

    Why questions call for an explanation, i.e., "Why does my cousin have this disease?" You would respond by searching for and indicating the reasons medical experts think that people get this disease.

    Which questions call for you to compare and contrast two or more situations, items, problems, solutions to problems, or answers to questions, etc., i.e., "Which sport should I play this fall?" You would respond by analyzing the pros and cons of several sports that interest you.

3. Questions that start with *who, what, when, where* will cover the factual information or descriptions surrounding your question or problem.

    Who else in my family has been adopted?

    What did my parents have to do to adopt me?

    When was I adopted?

    Where did my adoption take place?

Melissa's story illustrates the fascinating evolution of a student's thinking as she developed her pre-notetaking sheet. Melissa wanted to explore a topic related to young people with disabilities. She wrote on her pre-notetaking sheet:

> My friend ____ has Down's syndrome. I know it doesn't mean he lacks certain abilities. _____ has shown me that he is very active and able to do many things you wouldn't expect him to do. Some people with Down's syndrome are very capable, like Chris Burke, the TV actor in *Life Goes On*.

Working with an electronic database of journal articles, Melissa created potential research questions from the following key words and phrases: "causes," "care and treatment," "diagnosis," "genetics," "complications," and "risk factors." Her *What I Don't Know* list contained these and other questions: "What are the causes? When do you find out a child has Down's syndrome? How do doctors diagnose it? How do doctors care for and treat these children? What role does genetics play? What are some of the complications and risk factors?" Through individual conferencing with her media specialist and teacher and sharing her thoughts with peers, she discovered the questions she wanted to answer through her research: "How can people with Down's syndrome live 'normal' lives? What is 'normal'? Should children with this genetic disorder be in the same classroom with 'normal' students?" Her focus evolved from questions that could be answered with a few facts to questions about complex issues that required in-depth analysis.

Figure 4.5.   Sample: Melissa's Pre-notetaking Sheet

Pre-notetaking Sheet

Name: Melissa
Topic: Down's Syndrome

What I Know	What I Don't Know	What I Want to Know
1. One of my friends, ____ has Down's. I know it doesn't mean he lacks certain abilities. 2. ____ has shown me that he is very active and able to do many things you wouldn't expect him to do. 3. Some people with Down's are very capable. 4. Human chromosome 21 has something to do with this disorder. It has to do with genetics.	1. What are the causes? 2. When do you find out a child has Down's? How do doctors diagnose it? 3. How do doctors care and treat people with this syndrome? 4. What role does genetics play in this syndrome? 5. What are some of the complications and risk factors? 6. How does having Down's affect your personality? 7. Can students with Down's take classes with "normal" students? What is "normal"? 8. To what extent can people with Down's live normal lives? Work? Live alone? Have children? Raise a family? 9. Do people with Down's get embarrassed by it? 10. How do people react to those with Down's? How do people with Down's react to others?	1. Can people with Down's syndrome live "normal" lives—live alone, work, marry, have children? 2. Should children with this disorder be in the same classroom with "normal" children? What is "normal"? 3. How does having Down's syndrome affect your personality? 4. How are people with Down's treated by other people?

CONFERENCING DURING THE PRE-NOTETAKING STAGE USING BLOOM'S TAXONOMY

Conferencing with each student is essential after they complete initial drafts of their pre-notetaking sheets. During interventions at this stage, Bloom's *Taxonomy of Educational Objectives*, (1974) is a useful assessment tool. Most of the assessment will be based in the cognitive domain, which consists of six increasingly complex categories: *knowledge, comprehension, application, analysis, synthesis,* and *evaluation*. The chart in Figure 4.6 provides a summary of the taxonomy as presented in a companion guide to the *Information Skills Guide for Maine Educators* (1993, p. 28). The upper half of the chart defines the six levels of critical thinking (on the original Bloom's *Taxonomy* Chart) from the simplest to the most complex skills. The lower half suggests a list of words used to generate questions or create activities for each step in the hierarchy.

Figure 4.6.   Handout: Bloom's Taxonomy Chart

Bloom's Taxonomy Chart					
Knowledge Of	**Comprehension**	**Application of**	**Analysis**	**Synthesis**	**Evaluation**
Terms Facts Methods Procedures Concepts Principles	Uses implications Verbal to math Chart/graph Justify concept	Theory to practice Law to situation Problem solving Doing chart/graph	Recognize assumptions Recognize poor logic Distinguish fact Distinguish inference Evaluate relevancy Analyze structure	Write theme Present speech Plan experiment Integrates info	Consistency Data support Using standards Setting criteria
Remember Recall Define Describe Identify Label Match Name Outline Reproduce Select Underline List	Grasp meaning Explain Summarize Interpret Predict Paraphrase Translate Transpose format Retell Project Account for	Use in new situation Try Perform Develop Manipulate	Break into parts Re-organize Identify parts Analyze relationships Recognize patterns Examine Simplify Discern Compare Check Uncover Determine Assess	Create a new whole Present uniquely Propose a plan Establish Combine Produce Re-organize Formulate	Judge with purpose Decide Prioritize Classify Arbitrate Accept/reject Diagnose

An assessment of Melissa's work on Down's syndrome reveals the complexity and sophistication of her thinking. The earlier questions on her pre-notetaking sheet represent thinking at the lower level of the taxonomy: *knowledge* and *comprehension*. Later questions, however, reflect the upper range of the taxonomy. "What is 'normal'?" requires the *analysis* of various definitions of normalcy. To create her own, unique definition of the term, she has to *synthesize* concepts. "Should children with this disorder be in the same classroom with 'normal' children?" reveals thinking at the *evaluation* stage. Her pre-notetaking sheet demonstrates that she is capable of reaching the most complex stage of cognitive thinking.

In a teacher-student conference with Melissa, she reflects on where her questions fall on the taxonomy and has help explaining the significance of that placement. Her awareness of the taxonomy as a tool for creating questions that challenge her to think helps her transfer her question-making ability to other activities. Being aware of the depth of the research she wants to undertake gives her confidence. She is proud of her ability to think critically.

Because Melissa's pre-notetaking sheet needs no revision, the conference ends with a question: "What is your next step?" She shares her plans. Books are helping her answer some of her questions, but she also wants to interview _____ and members of his family. She also receives the suggestion that she interview the special education teacher in her school who works with two Down's syndrome students. She agrees that this is another good source of information and enthusiastically begins her work. Melissa uses excellent questions from her pre-notetaking sheet to focus her research journey and interview questions.

How do teachers and media specialists help students who encounter problems? Much of the success or failure of any research process depends on the quality of pre-search preparation and prior knowledge of the topic, especially if the topic is in the content area. In spite of the I-Search format, students whose background knowledge is inadequate or whose questions fail to involve higher-order thinking will still produce cut-and-paste products. Conferencing with these students needs to take the form of an intervention. The goal is to help them expand their background knowledge enough to create questions that promote critical thinking.

> The quality of pre-search preparation and prior knowledge of the topic determine much of the research success.

CONFERENCING TO HELP WITH QUESTION FORMATION

The next round of intervention conferencing comes after the general resource reading without notetaking and while students engage in producing a second pre-notetaking draft. Many students will still have difficulty creating good research questions.

Joyce works with a number of high school freshmen who complete I-Searches related to careers. They frequently have problems developing challenging research questions because their initial questions are usually factual in nature: What is the salary for this career? What skills do I need? Are there job openings in this field? What are the working conditions? What kind of education do I need?

Mike's story shows how conferencing can move a student from a consideration of factual information into the application of information to solve problems and make decisions. The conference began with Mike explaining the contents of his new pre-notetaking draft: "I selected my topic 'cause my father gave me books on welding and diving, and I really want to dive and weld. . . . I really want to be an underwater welder." This student already knew some details about his favored job.

For the *What I Don't Know* column, Mike created factual questions using information from general encyclopedias and a career handbook published by the United States Department of Labor. His interests included the skills he required for this job and the kind of education to make him competitive with other underwater welders. Because many of his questions were factual, the intervention consisted of posing questions to stimulate Mike's critical thinking, "How will you use your information to plan your career?" Mike thought he could compare the skills he already had with those needed by underwater welders. He would find his strengths and weaknesses and work to improve skills that were weak. Again, the intervention consisted of a question: "What is the first step in initiating this search plan?" After some thought, Mike decided that he should talk to his guidance counselor. To help Mike remember the decisions he made during the conference, he created new research questions, which he records in his *What I Want to Know* column: "What are my strengths and weaknesses? What can I do to improve my skills? How can my guidance counselor help me?" To conclude the conference, Mike received praise for his progress.

Reinforcement is an important element of the process, especially for a student like Mike, who described himself as someone who does not do well in school but can work beautifully with his hands as a carpenter. As a follow-up to the conference, Mike's English teacher asked him to review with her the previous decisions. He enjoyed sharing his pre-notetaking sheet with her because he was proud of its contents. His teacher is able to make an addition to the sheet by suggesting that Mike interview the welding instructor at the vocational school that resides at the high school. She offered to introduce Mike to the welding teacher.

Each intervention conference concludes with students and teacher or media specialists placing the student's questions at the appropriate level on the original Bloom's *Taxonomy Chart* (1974) to identify placement on the critical thinking hierarchy. Mike's conference would end with an explanation and analysis of how he had progressed with the quality of his questions, from *knowledge* and *comprehension* to *synthesis* (developing a plan of action) and *evaluation* (of his strengths and weaknesses). With the addition of this strategy, Mike would eventually gain a sense of the hierarchy of critical thinking and become a self-assessor of his critical thinking progress. He learned that he may revise or modify his questions later in the process. For many I-Searchers, the focus questions evolve as they gather new information. They will want to add new or revised questions to the *What I Don't Know* and the *What I Want to Know* columns.

REFLECTION ON THE PRE-NOTETAKING PROCESS

After drafting and revising the pre-notetaking sheet and conferencing with the media specialist and/or teacher, students take time to reflect on the process. The following questions help them craft a response in their learning logs:

1. Describe how the pre-notetaking sheet helped you find a focus for your topic and research questions to investigate.
2. Summarize what happened during your conference. What problems or obstacles did you identify during your conference? What strategies will you use to overcome them?
3. Evaluate your experience using the pre-notetaking sheet and your experience conferencing with your media spe-

cialist and/or teacher. How were these techniques useful? What suggestions would you make to improve these steps?

4. Now, what are you going to do next?

Have students read their responses to the class or share them with the members of their writing groups. Invite their peers to respond through class discussion or by writing brief responses to the students. Then, conduct a debriefing session posing the question: What conclusions can researchers draw about pre-notetaking and conferencing based on reflections?

The debriefing session identifies obstacles that still cause problems for students at this stage. Debriefing is a type of formative evaluation or ongoing assessment of the process and is critically important to the student and to the teaching team in analyzing the strategies students use in the process. Some students need extra time while others are ready to move on. If the teaching team modifies the timeline to keep the class together, they can facilitate future instruction at the point of need for all students. This stage of the process is a good place for a class break from the I-Search. Spending one or two days reading a short story, one-act play, or writing poetry provides a break from the intensity of the I-Search unit. It allows students who are somewhat behind to catch up before they go on to the next major strategy, e.g., those who decide to change topics.

> Debriefing identifies obstacles that still cause problems for students at this stage. Debriefing is a formative evaluation of the process.

FOCUSING ON RESOURCES

After finding a suitable focus and developing challenging research questions, students need time to focus on their resources. As a result, include time for reading, searching the Internet, viewing videos, searching electronic databases, and using multimedia computer programs. Students collect materials and apply information to their research questions. They experience an intense period of discovery with the excitement of finding information relevant to their questions. At this point, students bond with their topics.

The media center is the best place to work during this period. The students' hunger for resources is considerable. Thus, an atmosphere that is informal, yet controlled, encourages students to share their discoveries. Give them resource suggestions and ask them to talk about what they are doing.

At the end of each class session devoted to the investigation of resources, students reflect on the progress they make in their learning logs. Good probe questions that scaffold this process include the following:

- What new discoveries do they have?
- How do these discoveries influence their thinking?
- How do new connections that they make as a result of collecting new information inform their topic?
- Do they need to modify their action plan in light of new information?

Students periodically read past entries in their learning logs as a crucial part of the process. Short-term memory is fleeting. By reviewing their logs, they etch their insights into their long-term memory. If they need a reminder, the insight will be in their learning log. Reflection is one of the most powerful strategies in the I-Search process because of its relationship with critical thinking.

MAKING INFORMATION ACCESSIBLE

Students' experience with pre-notetaking sheet drafts and conferencing prevents most indiscriminate copying. Still, a few students will want to download and print mindlessly. In most cases, these students are still having problems articulating their focus. The next chapter discusses how students turn their information notes into their own reflective thinking about their topic through the double-entry draft strategy.

Pre-notetaking sheet drafts and conferencing prevents most indiscriminate copying.

INTERVIEWING AS AN ALTERNATIVE RESOURCE

The focusing period is a good time to seek out human resources and to schedule interviews. It is also a good time to schedule a lesson on interviewing techniques to calm students' hesitancies about the interviewing process. Some students know whom they want to interview and other students need suggestions of appropriate people. The student interested in Down's syndrome knew people who were "experts" on her topic. The underwater welder received suggestions from his teachers. Other students learned about human resources through their friends or through electronic databases.

Much of the planning for interviews takes place during conferencing or in a class session. It might help to review the following stages of the interview process and discuss answers to the corresponding questions with students:

1. Preparing for the interview
   a. How do you plan to make the appointment (e.g., by telephone, in person, or through an introduction performed by a third person)?
   b. What information should you know about the person being interviewed?
   c. What do you plan to accomplish during the interview?
   d. What questions do you plan to ask?
2. Conducting the interview
   a. What are the rules of etiquette for an interview (e.g., introductions, body language, listening skills, and thanking the interviewee)?
   b. How will you record information (e.g., taking notes or recording the conversation on audiocassette or videotape)?
   c. How do you obtain permission to tape an interview?
3. Following the interview
   a. Should you send a thank-you note?
   b. If questions arise as a result of new information, is a follow-up interview by phone or in person possible?

Technology is changing the methods students use to conduct interviews. Internet access facilitates e-mail interviews. Telephone interviews are another alternative, using an inexpensive microphone that fits between the ear and the telephone receiver to tape telephone interviews, if the interviewee grants permission. Some shyer students feel uncomfortable conducting person-to-person interviews. E-mail and fax interviews are good alternatives for these students. When the technology is not available, interviewing someone they know, such as a teacher, neighbor, or relative who might be an "expert" on their subject, is a possibility.

Interviews produce interesting results. With permission, the student studying Down's syndrome videotaped her interview of the Down's student and his family. She edited a copy of her videocassette so that she could share it with others. As a result of this interview and personal interactions with people having Down's syndrome, she became an advocate for individuals with disabilities. The student investigating underwater welding impressed the vocational instructor with his enthusiasm and knowledge. As a result, the instructor created a special program just for him. Mike started his vocational training as a second semester freshman instead of waiting until his junior year, the traditional time for students to join the vocational program. For these students, the I-Search is only a beginning. The next chapter discusses the search stage and addresses a plan of action for the research.

REFERENCES

Bloom, B. S. (1956). *Taxonomy of educational objectives: The classification of educational goals.* New York: Longmans, Green.

Bloom, B. S. (1974). *Taxonomy of educational objectives: The classification of educational goals.* New York: Longmans, Green.

Call, P. (1991). "SQ3R + what I know sheet = one strong strategy." *Journal of Reading, 35*(1), 50–54.

Maine Educational Media Association, Committee on Information Skills. (1993). *A Maine sampler of information skills activities for Maine student book award nominees, 1992–1993. Part 1.* Augusta, ME, Maine State Library.

Rankin, V. (1988). "One route to critical thinking." *School Library Journal, 34*(5): 28–31.

5 USING INFORMATION

Notecards! So necessary, yet so difficult for the teacher! Some students ask, "What do I do with all these notecards?" Or they exclaim, "Gee, haven't I done a good job! Look at how many notecards I've collected," expecting the highest form of praise from their teachers. But their papers are stunning in their demonstration of lack of insight and interpretation. Frequently, these students include a disturbing amount of information without concepts that pull the facts together. How strong are their strategies for assimilating their information, comprehending it, evaluating it, synthesizing it, and applying it? This chapter includes strategies for correcting this lack of skills and strategies.

CREATE A PLAN OF ACTION

Ask students to prioritize their resources in a manner that meets their information needs and facilitates their reading comprehension. If they are dealing with complicated subjects, they can arrange their resources in order of general to specific or in order of simplest in organization and writing style to more sophisticated in content and structure. Moving from general to specific and simple to complex increases students' comfort level with vocabulary and lets them gradually build their knowledge base, thus increasing their understanding of text. If they are dealing with controversial material or theories, they can group together authors with comparable ideas or opposing viewpoints. If they have a plan of action, they will make more discriminating and efficient use of information.

Placing the plan of action in their learning logs assures students constant access to remind them of the path they decide to follow in using their resources. It also reinforces reading strategies needed to comprehend increasingly difficult texts. Anytime they want to modify that plan, they note it in their learning log.

> A plan of action structures the research. Move from general to specific resources to build conceptual understandings.

HIGHLIGHT TEXT AND ADD MARGIN NOTES

Many teachers require students to use notecards as a strategy for choosing important pieces of information from a variety of sources, synthesizing the information, and organizing it into an original paper. Some students thrive on this method, but for others, information taken out of context loses its meaning. They fail to remember why they collected the isolated bits and pieces.

Students who cannot handle notecards try the strategy of highlighting text and adding margin notes. Students take photocopied materials they have gathered during their pre-search and then highlight important facts, potential answers to their research questions, phrases or sentences that produce a strong positive or negative reaction, and comparable and contradictory information found in other resources. They add marginal notes that provide a reminder of the reason for highlighting the text: "Author agrees/disagrees with [another author]," "That's disgusting!" "Excellent idea," "I predict," "Need more information on this," and other responses. These notes and the essential margin responses go into their learning logs in the form of double-entry drafts, which will be described later in this chapter.

Ask students to monitor their understanding of text. While students are reading, have them ask: What do I understand? What don't I understand? Then have them highlight unfamiliar vocabulary words and confusing portions of text and provide a marginal note explaining the nature of the problem. They work to "fix" their understanding when they write their reflections about their reading in their learning logs.

After highlighting text and writing marginal notes, students reflect on their experience in their learning log. Give them the following reading strategies to increase their understanding of text.

1. Have them summarize in their own words what they learned from the text. This helps them reflect on main ideas and supporting details.
2. Ask them to apply a variety of "fix up" strategies to check for understanding of confusing or difficult passages and vocabulary. "Fix up" strategies include:
    a. rereading a passage and paraphrasing it,
    b. asking a friend for help in understanding a word or section,

Monitoring comprehension is a key reading strategy. "Students who are good at monitoring their comprehension know when they understand what they read and when they do not. They have strategies to 'fix up' problems in their understanding as the problems arise." (CIERA, 2003, p. 56)

c. using context clues and analyzing parts of words (prefixes, roots, and suffixes) to determine meaning of unknown terms,

d. consulting a dictionary.

3. Have them include bibliographic information with their reflections, to insure that students remember the source.

4. Ask them to summarize the information that answers their research questions in a lively, first-person, narrative.

Problems with plagiarism seem to disappear with this strategy. However, intervention is sometimes necessary with students who have tendencies to highlight everything. Remind them to concentrate on material that answers their research questions.

DOUBLE-ENTRY DRAFTS

To encourage students to go beyond merely answering their research questions, have them evaluate their source using these criteria:

Ask students to evaluate their information for bias, reliability, and validity.

The learning log supports reading comprehension skills.

- currency;
- accuracy;
- point of view;
- bias, and;
- fact versus opinion.

Ask them also to reflect on how they feel when they connect new information to their personal experience and knowledge base. How does their thinking evolve as they move through Murray's (1980) process of collecting, connecting, writing, and reading? How is this information helping them solve problems or make decisions related to the topic that chooses them, to reach the itch that needs to be scratched? In the I-Search process, the answer is a technique developed by English teachers: the double-entry draft.

The double-entry draft is a tool that helps students make meaning from text. While most activities associated with the I-Search are taught through short lessons, double-entry drafting needs time for training.

Take time to give students skill in double-entry drafting.

It is a skill developed through practice, and needs monitoring to keep students progressing. When they first begin, their responses will be very brief. Practice will help them add details and depth of reflection to their responses. Prompts will help them move their comments to the upper levels of Bloom's *Taxonomy*. The following agenda will assist in a lesson design for teaching the double-entry draft:

DAY 1

Step 1: Demonstrate how to prepare the double-entry draft, and explain how to use it.

Directions: Divide a paper in half, lengthwise. Write the bibliographic information at the top of the page. Label the first column *Content* and the second column *Response* (Figure 5.1).

Figure 5.1. Template: Double-Entry Draft Format

Bibliographic   Information:

Content	Response

In the *Content* column, have students record a word, phrase, or one or two sentences that provoke a connection, or a positive or negative reaction. In the second column, ask them to explain their reaction. On the first day, each student focuses on making sense out of what he/she reads by relating it to personal experiences or personal knowledge of the topic. Possible response aids include, but are not limited to, the following:

- How does this idea connect to my question?
- How does this paraphrased passage relate to my question?
- What does this vocabulary word mean? (Ask them to look it up and summarize the context with their new meaning.)
- What is the meaning of this paragraph, sentence, or passage to my research?
- What personal experience does this passage remind me of? How might that experience connect to my question?
- What do I think about the author's writing style and why do I like or dislike it?

- What might I predict based on this evidence?
- How do I react to this information emotionally?
- What further questions does this information make me ask?

To aid students with the task, provide them with the following template. This template provides the format for content and corresponding responses.

Figure 5.2.   Sample: Double-Entry Draft Template with Probe Comments

Double-Entry Draft

Resource (Author, Title, etc.):

Content	Response
1. A main idea or key concept	1. Why it is a key point
2. A sentence/passage that produces a positive or negative reaction	2. An explanation of the reaction and the reason for that reaction
3. An unknown word	3. A possible definition
4. A confusing passage	4. A paraphrase of that passage
5. Questions that comes to mind	5. Reasons for wanting to know the answer or a possible answer
6. Information that relates to a personal experience	6. Personal experience
7. A statement of the author's opinion	7. Reasons for agreeing or disagreeing with the author
8. A key point	8. Another author's view on the same topic (comparison/contrast)
9. Important information	9. How the information helps to answer a research question
10. Other	10. Other

Model the process for creating double-entry drafts.

Step 2: Model the process described in Step 1.

Use an article from the local newspaper about an event of interest to the students. Read the article headline to the students, but do not read the text. Ask students briefly to discuss what they know about the topic covered by the article. Encourage them to think about and decide how much they know is factual or hearsay, or contains bias. This is a great opportunity to have them learn what bias means in a source and how it can affect the reliability and validity of the information.

Form students into groups to choose what question(s) they predict the article will answer. After noting the question(s) and creating a double-entry draft for each group, students follow along with their copy while one student reads the article aloud. Students use a pencil or pen to place a checkmark on their copy next to any parts of the text that produce a reaction. Working as a group, they write three of their examples of content and their responses to that content on a double-entry draft drawn on the smart board. Each group explains to the rest of the class how its choices inform the question. The other students brainstorm on how they perceive that the content answers the group's question. If the article is about a local, national, or international situation that interests students and they have some background knowledge in addition to the article, they should have additional interesting reactions to the content in relation to the question. When students make meaning of the text in relation to their essential question, they think critically about using information to answer questions or solve problems.

If the topic is controversial, encourage several minutes of lively debate about the content and student reactions to the content informing each group's question. All responses should be treated with value and respect, but open to discussion by all of the class. An additional exercise would be to have the class prioritize the importance of the information chosen to each question.

At the end of the period, debrief the students. First show them how to write the proper bibliographic citation for the article. Then ask them whether the activity was meaningful as well as useful. Ask each student to reflect on a separate sheet of paper how they would use the double-entry draft to focus on the essential information in a resource related to their question or problem. How might this strategy prevent them from taking notes about information not useful for their problem-solving?

"Effective comprehension strategy instruction can be accomplished through cooperative learning. . . . Students work together to understand content-area texts, helping each other learn and apply comprehension strategies." (CIERA, 2003, p. 60)

DAY 2

Step 3: During this period, it is time to introduce or reinforce strategies for evaluating information. Choose another article on

<table>
<tr><td>

Introduce strategies for evaluating information for reliability and validity.

</td></tr>
</table>

the same topic covered in the previous period, preferably from a different source. Then give students the following evaluative questions to answer that address the information they've chosen from the article. They work with the same group partners and use the same essential question they created during the previous period. Their focus will be on evaluating the information for reliability and validity.

- Is the information current?
- What is the author's purpose, e.g., informative or persuasive?
- What is the author's point of view?
- Is the author biased?
- Does the information in the article agree or disagree with other sources? Give examples.
- Is the author and/or publisher reliable? What is their reputation?
- How do the graphics (pictures, charts, graphs, photos) contribute to an understanding of the information?
- Is the author's presentation logical? Explain.
- Does the author support his/her generalizations with facts and examples? Justify your response.

If students demonstrate interest in the topic, they will get into lively debates about these questions. When they come together as a class, hopefully, they will ask such questions as how a reader could know whether an author is biased and how a reader could find out about the author's authority. Students will want to know how newspapers or magazines validate the credibility of their sources before they publish an article. Perhaps they will ask, "What is the difference between an editorial allowing opinions and a story printed on the other pages?" Answers to these queries should have students asking about how much they can believe and when they should read text as someone else's opinion.

DAY 3

The lively debate creates a situation where students start using thinking skills to analyze, synthesize, question, and evaluate the information they have. At this point, give them another newspaper article on the topic (clearly, collecting the appropriate articles will take some foresight). While students analyze the articles, ask them to look for the inclusion of opposing points of view and explain how that inclusion leads to more balanced coverage. They will want to know when opposing viewpoints are not appropriate, e.g., when the author has a responsibility to report an event and does not need to include a balanced perspective. If one of the articles they have is an editorial, they might confuse opinion with facts. This is a good time for differentiating conceptually between opinion and fact so that they understand.

Have them create their own double-entry drafts and compare them as a class. They should discover several different interpretations of the same material among their groups. Ask them to discuss and share with the class why each interpretation has value and can lead to more understanding about answering questions and solving problems. There is usually more than one way to answer a research question or more than one solution to a problem. In fact, this is where the difference among individuals becomes apparent, when thinking critically about how the same information informs a question or problem. They now see why each researcher is responsible for questioning the validity and reliability of the information they use and its source. Given two individuals observing the same event, each individual will write about the "facts" as he or she experiences them. Given two individuals reading the same information to answer the same question, they might each interpret the information as answering the question differently. This is the time to stress the lack of definitive answers for most of life's events, questions, and problems. Answers rarely come from textbooks or are ready-made. Students need these critical thinking tools in order to form their own perspectives. Thus, their essential questions, if higher-order, will not have answers that come from cut-and-pasted material, but will require digging and thinking.

Finally, have students use the following homework assignment to practice and apply what they learn in class:

> When do newspaper articles contain opinion and when do they need to be factual reporting? When do articles need to contain opposing viewpoints?

FOLLOW-UP ASSIGNMENT ON DOUBLE-ENTRY DRAFTING

1. Select an article you have already prioritized on your resources list.
2. Complete a double-entry draft from your choice, noting at least two pieces of information you think informs your question. Write a personal reaction to each information choice. Include your evaluation of the information for reliability and validity.
3. Write an entry in your learning log about how the double-entry draft helps you understand what you are reading and apply it to your question.

4. Submit your learning log (including the double-entry draft) to your media specialist or teacher for comments on your progress.

Monitor the early double-entry drafts, especially the first draft done independently, to assess students' critical thinking skills. Write reactions to student responses in the form of questions designed to challenge student thinking. For example, follow a brief, undeveloped response with a request for more details. Using Bloom's *Taxonomy*, push student responses to a higher level of critical thinking with question probes.

> Use Bloom's *Taxonomy* to analyze double-entry draft responses.

MOVE FROM DOUBLE-ENTRY DRAFTS TO LEARNING LOGS

What to write when extending double-entry draft reflections to learning log narrative responses sometimes baffles even graduate students. However, a learning log narrative entry after each new double-entry draft is the primary tool for evaluating, synthesizing, and organizing how the double-entry draft responses inform the essential question or subquestions. It also provides students with an opportunity to check for their understanding of the text, an important reading strategy for monitoring comprehension. The entries facilitate meaning-making from the double-entry thoughts and responses to what students read. Because such thoughts and reflections arise as a result of attaching the new double-entry draft reflections to the students' prior knowledge about their topic, students have a natural, progressive organization of their final product already in progress through their learning log narrative. They reflect on their successes or failures in their information search as part of what they discover. They reflect on the reliability and validity of the factual information they collect, comparing and contrasting it with other resources. They state their own perspectives about how the new material informs their questions.

The learning log narrative essentially becomes the text that they will use in their final product. Instead of facing that barrier of how they should write the final paper and relying on other authors' words, much of their paper exists in their learning log narrative. The I-Search's use of first-person narrative in the final product honors their writing as thinkers and authors.

Students transfer their writing to their final product after organizing it in the structure they want for their final product. This is

> A learning log entry after each double-entry draft is a primary tool for evaluating, synthesizing, and applying double-entry draft responses to the essential question. The learning log narrative becomes the text for the final product.

"Good readers use metacognitive strategies to think about and have control over their reading." (CIERA, 2003, p. 55)

the time they go back to their pre-notetaking sheet where they have the various subquestions to their essential question and use them as section headings. Their reflections that respond to each of their subquestions form the narrative for their paper. It helps if they can practice writing a summarizing paragraph for the section that pulls all their thoughts together in a response to the question. Once they have organized their responses to each subquestion, then they can write a conclusion synthesizing how the subquestions inform and answer the essential question.

Angie's story is an example of how a student successfully moves from the double-entry draft to the learning log. It reveals and illustrates how double-entry drafts help her make sense of text and alerts the media specialist and classroom teacher to any comprehension problems.

Angie became interested in the Supreme Court decision *Roe v. Wade* after discussing important U.S. Supreme Court cases in her history class. She knew about the controversy over abortion because of the demonstrations in her hometown of Bangor, Maine. She knew little about the court cases related to it.

After reading a chapter from her history text, Angie took notes and created a double-entry draft responding to the text's description of the *Roe v. Wade* case and its legal precedent, *Connecticut v. Griswold.* Taking her responses from her double-entry draft, Angie used them to summarize the case and explain the outcome. She also used a quote from the text which she has in her double-entry draft, the key sentences from the majority opinion written by Justice William O. Douglas: "We would [*sic*] allow the police to search the sacred precincts of marital bedrooms for telltale signs of use of contraceptives? The very idea is repulsive to the notions of privacy surrounding the marriage relationship."

Angie's double-entry draft content notes revealed a basic understanding of what is important about the case, and they also revealed a potential reading comprehension problem: "I agree with the decision of the court in the aspect that the police had no right to go into married couples [*sic*] bedrooms and go through their stuff." Was Angie interpreting Justice Douglas's remarks literally? A follow-up conference revealed that Angie's problem related to her schema. A viewer of television shows such as *Cops,* she interpreted the quote using her vision of the criminal court system as one where police search a home to find evidence. Working with Angie helped her understand the difference between the criminal justice system and judicial review. After the conference, she wrote about what she learned from the text and the conference in her learning log. This helped her reinforce the concepts from the conference. Analysis of her double-entry journal and the resulting conference proved necessary to correct misconceptions that inhibited Angie's understanding of text.

As Angie moved from her double-entry drafts her to learning log, she connected her new learning to the world around her. One of Angie's early learning logs is a powerful example of what happens when students connect their life experiences with content area learning:

> Today I photocopied pages from a legal book, *Roe v. Wade: The Abortion Question,* by D.J. Herda. It talks about the *Roe vs. Wade* case. The first thing that caught my eye was a big picture of Norma McCorvey, otherwise known as Jane Roe.
>
> I never knew a thing about this case. I've always heard it mentioned, but I never knew it was about abortion. It's interesting because abortion now is an important subject in society today. I remember yesterday driving through downtown. People were holding up signs of bloody babies, saying abortion kills. But you can drive up the street and see people for abortion. I am not sure. It all should depend on the situation. The other day my mom was watching a movie where a girl didn't want her parents to find out she was pregnant so she had an illegal abortion, got sick, and died because of it. It was sad and showed people to be aware of the situations going on. I think it will be very interesting reading about and researching this case.

Through her learning log narrative, Angie demonstrated one of Maine's Learning Results standards related to reading by connecting her life experiences to her content area learning. She explained how new information from a text changed her personal knowledge. Most importantly, she grappled with social issues surrounding local abortion protests and counter-demonstrations at a local hospital and a women's health center. She experienced first-hand how social and political climates influenced the court's decision.

The I-Search experience encouraged Angie to form her own conceptual understandings about the problem. She strengthened her use of resources and comprehension of the material through her practice in evaluating resources for bias, reliability, and validity. Her reading comprehension skills increased through her reflective writings in her double-entry drafts and learning log entries. If Angie did not move to a deeper level of critical thinking through her reflections, she might not so easily interpret what she was reading through her life experiences. Her first-person narrative voice allowed her to express her thoughts in her natural language, making meaning of her thoughts available to herself and to her readers without the complications of forced third-person format.

SCAFFOLD LEARNING LOG REFLECTIVE ENTRIES

Josh's story shows the evolution of thinking as he moved from his research questions to the double-entry draft to the learning log entry. Josh is a precocious young student interested in extrasensory (ESP) perception. At first his teacher tried to convince him to select a more personal topic, but he persuaded her that this was a valid subject for a student with a strong interest in science. Before his first conference with his teacher, however, his research questions stayed at the *knowledge* and *comprehension* levels: "What are some of the tests for ESP? Are there different tests for different types of ESP?" With the support of his teacher, Josh revised his questions: "What is the difference between science and pseudoscience? Do scientists who measure ESP have an accurate way of measuring ESP? Does ESP really exist? Is it a valid scientific phenomenon?" These questions reflected analysis and evaluation that required him to develop criteria for judging a scientific phenomenon. Below is an early entry from Josh's learning log:

> I then read *ESP* by Michael Arvey, a short book from the *Great Mysteries Series* (1989). I learned about Dr. J. B. Rhine of Duke University. He [is] one of the first to initiate serious attempts to study ESP. One experiment he devised was the use of cards. These cards, Zener cards, are blank on one side and have one of five symbols printed on the other, either a cross, a circle, a star, a square, or wavy lines. Rhine's test was quite easy. Each ESP candidate would be asked to "guess" the symbol on randomly selected cards, without seeing it. . . . I was very surprised to read about one of Rhine's subjects, Adam Linzmeyer, who correctly answered 119 out of 300. The odds of doing that are about 75,000 to 1. Another of Rhine's tests involved PK or psychokinesis. Psychokinesis defined is the ability to move matter by just

one's mind. Rhine tested to see if people could willfully influence the way dice fell when rolled. This book also talked about how Rhine's work has been really criticized by critics. Some criticism came from his subjects being able to see through the Zener cards. Also, Rhine's fascinating outcomes have never been duplicated by other researchers.

Without criticizing Josh's original content, or expressing concern about writing or spelling errors, his teacher wrote the following response in the margin of his learning log: "Good beginning! You are finding answers to your research questions. As for the criticism of Rhine's work, this brings out an important point. How does one discover criteria to test for scientific validity? How can one judge whether or not a scientist has devised an experiment that produces accurate results? Perhaps one of the science teachers can help you answer these questions." This response marked the beginning of a written dialogue between teacher and student as Josh addressed the questions. When he demonstrated critical thinking by articulating ideas and concepts, his teacher withheld attention to writing errors until the draft of the final I-Search paper.

E-mail improves the teacher and media specialist's ability to use conferencing as a check for student progress and a vehicle for communication to assist students with their journey. When students in a class have e-mail accounts, the teaching team opens an I-Search class dialogue using e-mail, creates workgroups for support, and makes itself more available for individual student help. The value of conferencing during the I-Search project increases when more time can be spent outside of class.

Angie and Josh's stories lead to the important final stage of the I-Search process: the written paper or other type of product, which not only gives students one last opportunity to review and evaluate their work, but evolves into a finished product suitable for student publication and/or presentation. The next chapter contains suggestions for final products.

> If a student demonstrates critical thinking, wait to critique grammar, format, and spelling until the final product draft.

REFERENCES

Center for the Improvement of Early Reading Achievement (CIERA). (2003). *Put reading first: The research building blocks of reading instruction.* 2nd ed. Partnership for Reading. Retrieved August 19, 2005, from http://www.nifl.gov/partnershipforreading/publications/Cierra.pdf

Murray, D. M. (1982). "Writing as process: How writing finds its own meaning." In Murray, D. M. *Learning by teaching: Selected articles on writing and teaching.* (pp. 17–31) Portsmouth, NH: Heinemann.

PRESENTING THE PRODUCT AND ASSESSING THE PROCESS

THE FINAL PRODUCT

The format for the I-Search final product is flexible but should fit the nature of the question or problem.

Although Macrorie (1988) envisioned the I-Search as a paper, it lends itself to final products in a variety of formats. Other types of products, give teachers the opportunity to stress critical thinking and information literacy skills that transfer to more traditional research paper assignments. Papers, computer software presentations, oral presentations, photo albums, genealogies, diaries, action plans, letters, agendas, design drawings, etc., provide excellent opportunities for students to apply their critical thinking to answering essential questions and solving problems in a clear, well supported process. No matter what the final product, the I-Search process promotes use of critical thinking resulting in transformative learning, which is learning that stays with the student and transforms the student's perspective. One of the joys in an I-Search unit is the chance to encourage students to find the presentation format that fits their question or problem effectively and efficiently. All of these products require the pre-search and search strategies, which demonstrate student skills in reading, writing, thinking, and reasoning abilities.

Conferences during the process offer opportunities to convey formative assessments to students at critical points designated prior to the start of the I-Search unit. The assessments inform you when you need to scaffold students at that point in the process. Stopping students before they move to the following step enables you to strengthen students' skills in problem areas. The success of the I-Search depends on cumulative step successes. If students skip or slide over some of the strategic steps, their final product displays the lack of those steps. This process places as much or more value on formative process assessments as it does on a summative product assessment. The flexibility is there to assess in a multitude of ways.

Whatever the final product, the I-Search presents a unique opportunity for students to discover their natural writing abilities. It is a process that builds confidence in writing because it promotes the use of naturalistic language through first-person narrative that conveys the students' own reflective, critical thinking about their topics.

Writing in first person gives students a chance to write about their feelings and tell the story of their search from their own perspective, formed by thinking critically about the topic. For the first time, students who have writer's block discover the fun of telling their audience what they find and how it relates to their question or problem and to themselves. When the iterative nature of the I-Search process strengthens their research skills, students know they can improve and revise their content and essential questions. The ability to express their own perspective and opinions about the topic takes away the pressure to present a factual recitation that is stiff and unnatural, and probably a paste-up of others' ideas. The teaching team receives strong satisfaction from watching students respond to other students' appreciation of what they have to say and how they say it. Their confidence and new self-esteem permeates their discussion about their experience.

> Using naturalistic language through first-person narrative makes it easier for students to convey their critical thinking.

USE THE LEARNING LOG TO CREATE A FINAL PAPER

The final product can be an edited version of the learning log, if you choose, especially if this project is the students' first I-Search experience. This means that they will already have essentially written their final product after they have collected evidence and reflections through their double-entry drafts and synthesized them in learning log entries. Imagine the satisfaction when they comprehend what they have done. Imagine the new confidence when they already have a strong idea about the success of their I-Search because they have satisfied a personal need. Grades take on a lesser importance.

Because their learning logs contain their thoughts, reflections, and notes from their reading, it is their record of their search strategies, including their reflections on the usefulness of each strategy to their search. It contains how they think and respond to their question and how they react to various I-Search strategies. Before they submit the final product, the teaching team can predict its quality.

Because student learning logs start with their initial personal webs and their research questions, they have a record of their reflective thoughts throughout their I-Search: why the topic chose them and what they want to discover. Their learning logs also document their thoughts and reflections on their experiences during the I-Search process, what they find, how they apply their findings, and their feelings about their final answers. The learning log is a realistic and valuable tool to help students move from seemingly unrelated source notes to a product that takes a fresh look at a topic through their eyes.

To help students edit the writing in their learning log, ask them to create a sequential web or an outline of the questions and reflections in the order of importance informing their essential question. The linear learners gravitate toward the outline and the visual learners use the web. This strategy supports their ability to organize their material and find places to fit major pieces in a logical response. The resulting product is a process evolution of how they answer their question. It is the story of their search.

The heart of the I-Search, as intended by Macrorie (1988), is the first-person narrative. Thus, it is evident that the first-person narration in their learning logs that expresses their thoughts and feelings from a personal viewpoint, should transfer easily to the final product. Permission to use natural language means that students do not have to worry about changing to a third-person perspective when they try to convey their interpretations and applications of information to problem-solving. For many students, first-person narrative eliminates the final product writing block that seems to encourage cutting and pasting factual information. The teaching team has the added bonus of receiving products that are exciting, interesting, and challenging. Observing the students' growing sophistication and knowledge about their topics through the I-Search process is a treat in itself.

Unfortunately, by middle school, students have already been acclimated to the necessity of eliminating the first-person perspective in research writing. Students have been taught that "I think" and "I feel" are taboo to use in research. They have a difficult time thinking reflectively in first person, and trusting that their critical thinking is imperative for the success of their I-Search. These students will fight the idea of having to do a research product because it is so unnatural to them. Even so, some of them will need extra support before they understand the I-Search and your expectations. Freedom to work on topics and questions that interest them, even within the content area, will be a first-time event for many students.

Topic choice is critical with these students. Helping them value their ideas on a subject is easier if they have ownership of their topics. If they are interested, they will search out the information to solve a problem. An academic topic, "hot" topic, or problem that is assigned to them will probably dampen their motivation to pur-

True ownership of topics helps students value their ideas.

Watch for students who want to switch from first-person investigative narrative to third-person reporting of facts.

sue information resources and apply what they find to their question. When they truly own their topic, i.e., a topic chooses them or they choose an interest area within a curriculum topic, they will apply the information they find to make sense of their question. Learning comes when they reflect and write in their learning logs about the information they find and how they think it will inform their question. Their learning logs demonstrate the depth of their interest and enthusiasm. Their reflections demonstrate their critical thinking about the search experience and synthesis of information as it applies to their question. They should be ready to transfer their comments to a final product quite easily, depending on requirements for the format of the final product.

Watch for the students who want to switch from the first-person point of view in their writing back to third-person reporting of the information they find. They have had experience with the latter and it may seem more comfortable. Students might not believe that the teaching team wants them to write in the first person, regardless of how many times they are told this. Many will start off using the first person, but revert back to a traditional third-person report; or, they will use the third-person style all the way through their writing, unless the teaching team spots it in their learning logs and supports the transition to first person via prompts. The log provides an opportunity to intervene before the problem becomes a hindrance to their ability to think critically about how their information informs their question. The first-person narrative requirement sometimes proves an obstacle for students who write papers that only report facts.

The following question prompts assist students who have problems writing in the first person. Ask them:

- How do you feel about this material?
- How does this information apply to you?
- What do you think the author means by this statement or passage?
- What ideas have you had about this topic?

These are the same questions to use in scaffolding students having trouble relating the information to a problem. Give them time to revise without penalty.

PEER EDITING

Macrorie (1988) stresses peer editing as a strategy that improves student writing quality. Peer editing gives students a chance to help each other by asking questions to develop and improve these facets of their writing:

- clarity,
- spelling and grammatical errors,
- additional ideas or approaches the writer had not considered, and
- passages where the writer is reporting rather than narrating in first person.

Peer editing is a strong information literacy skill that makes use of analytical and evaluative critical thinking. Peer editors ask for clarification and respond to choices of problem-solving techniques, opinions, and information application. Their suggestions about writing and presentation help writers express what they want to say. While they are editing, students learn new information and how to become better writers. They take pride in their editing efforts because they make their peers' products stronger.

Peer editing is difficult for most students, from middle school to graduate school. Many students fail to edit credibly when they think they will hurt the author's feelings. When this happens, stress the techniques for editing, the value of editing, and also depersonalize the writers' products. Editing is not about the writer but about improving the product. In this situation, ask students to take the perspective that the peer editor does not criticize but rather gives suggestions and catches errors.

Stress to the students that they are peer editors who can best support their fellow students by using the following techniques:

- highlighting redundant material;
- questioning confusing passages that need clarification;
- suggesting alternative word choices;
- checking for readability and lengthy sentences;
- identifying where writers could strengthen their evidence;
- checking for paragraph organization; and
- proofing the paper or product for proper usage of format, spelling, grammar, and mechanics.

Peer editing supports content learning as well as enhancing the writing and research process. Students working with their writing partners accumulate a wealth of information on topics they might never research but can apply to their lives and to schoolwork. For example, a student editing an I-Search on the connection of Rachel Carson to marine biology learned about genetics through her peer's paper. Through peer editing, content knowledge spreads effectively and efficiently from one student to another in the context of the real world. If students choose topics that are personally important, their peers will appreciate the value of the content and tend to remember it.

ADAPTABILITY TO A VARIETY OF GRADE LEVELS

One pleasure of the I-Search is its adaptability for use at multiple academic levels. Articles in *English Journal* and other journals for teachers indicate a wide variety of interpretations in using the I-Search. Teachers and media specialists modify and adapt I-Search strategies for first graders up to university graduate students. They adapt the techniques to the degree of students' cognitive development and preparedness. They do not hesitate to add or subtract strategies according to learning goals and objectives. Experience indicates that the I-Search at any level is a method that improves information literacy as it increases content knowledge, problem-solving, decision-making, writing abilities, and presentation skills.

The accompanying CD-ROM contains I-Search units included in this text, as well as others, as examples of the flexibility and adaptability of the process. If class time and the curriculum requirements do not allow for a topic choice I-Search or a content area I-Search, the individual strategies will work in other units where they enhance student learning growth. The key to higher-order thinking about their topics is to have students reflect on what they are doing and how they are finding and applying their information to their topic question. Writing about their reflective thinking ensures that their thoughts make their way into their long-term memory.

Peer editing spreads content learning.

The I-Search is adaptable to all grades.

OPTIONS FOR PRESENTATIONS

The I-Search strategies increase alternative assessment opportunities, as well as teach strong research fundamentals, and adapt as a group or individually to fit learning goals. For example, if one of the objectives is to have students acquire or strengthen computer literacy skills that enable a variety of presentation formats, ask them to create their final presentation as a Microsoft PowerPoint program or a multimedia product. Check to make certain that the topics and essential questions present effectively in the chosen format. If the goal is to increase their visual literacy, encourage students to use a digital camera and a photography editing program to prepare their graphics for insertion into a Word document, slide show, PowerPoint presentation, or a realia product such as a scrapbook.

Whatever the final product choice, the quality of the product will demonstrate the level of student motivation and interest in the topic. Meaningful essential questions keep students involved and thoughtful. The depth of their use of information resources to aid their thinking will be obvious in the presentation of their decision-making reasons.

Do not be surprised at the excitement students have when they become the expert in their area of investigation. If they present orally at the end of the I-Search, rare will be the students who do not enjoy sharing their learning experience and what they found out in the process. Confidence in their knowledge of their subject will be evident to the class, as the class asks questions about the topic and treats the student as the expert. Pride in work will also increase as peers express their interest in the student's I-Search.

With this kind of positive environment, spurring a discussion about what the students learn in their I-Searches happens easily. Form a circle and have all speakers remain seated during their presentations. This format helps everyone relax and participate, instead of having only the speaker do the talking. It doesn't seem as if the speaker is lecturing about the topic. If, by chance, a student forgets his/her material, offer a question or ask other students for a question. That usually gets the speaker started again. Because of conferencing, you know the material and will already have questions that will set the presenter at ease. Asking the student to tell the story of his/her search provides a natural organization that helps make material interesting. Most students respond positively to this environment.

> The quality of the product demonstrates interest and motivation of the student.

EFFECT ON STUDENTS' LIVES

The best personal I-Searches continue to affect students' lives long afterward. Students who investigate careers as their I-Search know what to expect and how to prepare, as well as get a better sense of whether they will like the career. Students who investigate family illnesses or their own medical problems come away with a far greater understanding of how they can help themselves or their family members take control of the problem. As an asthma sufferer, Jason was shocked to find several articles in weekly newsmagazines noting an increase in asthma deaths. Could the cause be medication prescribed by doctors? "I knew this was my topic!" Jason said in his learning log. "At first I was concerned that the information I would find might scare me a bit, and I would become overly concerned with death. After giving it a lot of consideration, I stuck with it."

By carefully comparing and contrasting facts and opinions from newsmagazines and the newsletter *Asthma Today,* Jason discovered the real cause of the deaths: human error. He found that sometimes patients are at fault because they fail to follow their doctors' orders. Sometimes the doctors are at fault because they do not give patients adequate explanations of how to care for themselves and use their medications. Jason concluded: "Overall, I believe that most deaths are preventable, and most are the result of carelessness by patient and physician. If people just kept up with the latest medicines and used them properly . . . asthma deaths would greatly be reduced."

But his story did not end with his I-Search. During his interview with his doctor and subsequent office visits, Jason asked his doctor questions. As a result, Jason reported that, "My doctor was so impressed with what I knew, he really opened up to me. . . . Now my doctor spends more time with me. He explains my treatment in detail." Jason was not the only student whose search continued beyond the teaching unit. The underwater welder implemented a plan for gaining skills needed for a challenging career. The student who studied Down's syndrome became an advocate for students diagnosed with disabilities.

Another student preparing for college knew she needed scholarship help in order to attend. She was skillful in tennis, and with the help of her mother, prepared a video of her play in competition. Her I-Search helped her discover how to prepare a presentation for college coaches to get them interested in her play. Her I-Search also helped her choose the kinds of colleges that appealed to her academically, residentially, and by size, as well as having scholarships available for women's tennis team members. This I-Search had a considerable influence on her college career.

The young student in Soweto, South Africa, who learned the I-Search strategies, will be forever memorable. Watching his face as he soaked up the strategies was like seeing someone suddenly realizing that he could face decisions about important life questions, now that he knew how to research them effectively. He exclaimed one day at the last workshop he attended, that he was learning a life process, not something just for school. His facial expression was unforgettably filled with pride.

AUTHENTIC ASSESSMENT

The I-Search easily lends itself to authentic assessment, formative and summative. Stripling (1995) defines *authentic assessment* as having a real-life context. Authentic assessment has several important components:

- a learning experience for students,
- ongoing throughout the learning process,
- based on real-life content, and
- involves reflection by both student and teacher.

Authentic assessment gives feedback to students in the form of conferencing, reflection, peer review, and evaluation based on process. The components of the I-Search fit the requirements of authentic assessment naturally and effectively.

Elements of the authentic assessment definition are interwoven throughout the I-Search process within the strategies, conferencing, reflective writing, and critical thinking in learning logs. Students invest in topics that they relate to their interests and/or life situations and that have the potential to affect their lives. Reflection continually takes place through learning logs and questioning techniques. Using the learning logs as a tool for communication, the teaching team responds to students' thinking, information analysis, and application of information to their questions. They provide suggestions and guidance when students stumble or need help for any reason, such as choosing a more effective alternative strategy or switching to another essential question. They are giving students an authentic assessment when they check their progress through their learning logs and tell them where they need to strengthen their use of a particular strategy

> Authentic assessment is formative and summative within:
> - strategies,
> - conferencing,
> - reflective writing,
> - critical thinking in the learning logs, and
> - final product.

before they continue to the next step. The assessment comes in the form of conferencing without students feeling that they are failing or have no opportunities to improve their efforts.

Students will usually have some prior knowledge of topics that relate to their lives or their interest areas, contributing to a natural list of questions they want to answer. This authentic environment encourages collaboration among students through discussion of their topics, peer questioning, and peer editing of each other's work. Students involve themselves by helping each other solve problems and make decisions through their suggestions. Logs and conferencing techniques provide students a platform for reflecting and answering such questions.

All of these elements are also present when the I-Search is in a content area. The major modification is that the topic and essential question are derived from the designated content area. If students use the other strategies applicable to topic choice and essential question-making, they will have a considerable element of choice in a topic that appeals to them. If you assign an I-Search project in a specific content area, give students enough background information to pique interest in the topics. Participate with them in brainstorming interesting topics and questions as a class. Then have them web two or three areas of interest. You set the parameters of the interest areas according to your content goals, but you can still give students a choice of what interests them. Brainstorming with students on how this content area influences their lives outside the classroom helps them situate the topic. Depending on the unit's objectives, as much topic choice as possible will help students make the process transferable to other research projects.

Perhaps, one of the most authentic environment elements is the need for students to organize their research agenda and build their task management skills to handle the flexibility built into the process approach. Students quickly learn that they have to use their time constructively and finish steps in the process at a regular pace to avoid frustration at the end and a poorer quality product. No longer is the overnight paper a possibility. Formative conference assessments keep students on track and catch those who might otherwise fall through the cracks and find themselves pasting together a last-minute effort. Students who are personally involved with their topic have a stronger desire to make steady progress in the research process and, many times, do not want to give up their research. They will even ask for time to work on their I-Search during any lulls in class activities. If each student receives a checklist of important indicators of progress, they will know what you expect when you read their learning logs. The checklist will be very helpful in facilitating your attention to students who need support.

This checklist also plays a part in the flexibility of the I-Search process and authentic assessment environment. Some students might need more practice with skills or strategies that counter their usual habits. The kinds of difficulty students meet frequently depends on the nature of topics they choose. Some topics will require more outside resources and interviews, while other topics will have sufficient information in the media center and on the Internet. The learning log that contains double-entry drafts facilitates your ability to spot students who need more support reflecting on the information they gather. If their reflections are weak, they will have greater difficulty answering their question, utilizing their own critical thinking, and transitioning from the learning log to a final product.

The I-Search includes these techniques for authentic assessment:

- rubrics for student reflection,
- peer review,
- ongoing conferencing,
- process assessment, and
- student self-assessment of the product, process, and experience.

Rubrics are scoring guides that describe what varying degrees of mastery or quality look like for each step or component (Redding, 1994, p. 132). One of the strengths of the I-Search is that students believe that the content of the final product belongs to them; thus, assessment of content would take a different form from traditional papers. Instead of looking for quality topic coverage, assess the product by how students use information to inform their decision-making or solve a problem.

> Checklists allow the teaching team to track students who need extra support.

ASSESSMENT SUGGESTIONS

Regardless of the final product's format, consider assessing process and content by using levels of Bloom's *Taxonomy* (1974). Use the following tools for assessing process:

- student reflective comments,
- observations,
- conferencing,

- timeline checklist, and
- performance checklist.

There are also the traditional means of writing quality assessments for all steps of the process.

CONTENT

Use questions to aid assessment.

Consider using these questions when assessing content and in determining the degree of the student's accomplishments (effectively, satisfactorily, needs improvement):

- Do the learning log and final product display factual accuracy based on a reasonable number and mixture of sources that the student compares and contrasts? (A "reasonable number" will vary by topic.)
- Do students base their problem-solving decisions on an effective analysis of the information they collect during the I-Search?
- Does the content of the learning log and final product demonstrate the student's comprehension and understanding of the topic through reflective thinking?
- Does the student present, compare, and contrast more than one approach to solving the problem?
- Does the student present arguments from several perspectives and synthesize them into the student's own perspective?

The I-Search creates a different aura around the content that seems to defy traditional assessment of content. Because of topic choice, students choose and own their content and make decisions about what that content should contain. Assessing students' use of information for problem-solving, its accuracy, and its relationship to the problem provides the tool for emphasizing that the content has to be of a high quality and fulfill the demands of the student's essential question. How they answer their question is their decision but they need to base their answer on quality use of information from a mix of resources and give good reasons for their answer. Require them to be accurate and justify their choices of information. Ascertain that they have investigated validity and reliability of the information they use, as evidenced through their reflective comments on their double-entry drafts and in their learning logs. If they fulfill these criteria for finding, using, and applying information to their question and can defend it, it will be easy to appreciate the thinking they have done (even if there is disagreement with their conclusion). If they arrive at a factually inaccurate answer to their question, look at their process and see where they have a problem. What step did they miss or slight? If they arrive at a surprising perspective, look at their process to understand their thinking. If it is the result of critical thinking recorded in their journal, they deserve credit. The personal nature of the I-Search grants them that privilege.

PROCESS

The following questions assess process and product. Some of the questions cover formative assessments during the process. To address the important parts of the process, divide the questions into three categories: *pre-search, search,* and *presentation.* Ask questions about writing quality at the level of question-making, double-entry drafting, learning log writing, and final product. If the final product is a paper, critique all the writing products for a complete assessment. Whatever the product format, look for natural language, effective use of the first-person narrative, and use of higher-order verbs when describing how the data answer the question. Sentence construction, spelling, and grammar are not factors at this level. The overall product assessment can include these criteria after peer editing.

Share the following assessment tool with the students at the beginning of the unit to let them know the evaluation criteria. These questions assist students in checking their progress throughout the I-Search. The questions are particularly useful in the final conference, when students can explain their process. Letting students articulate what they think happens in their research solidifies the strengths of the process and assignment in their minds. Alternatively, have them finish their learning logs with these questions, stimulating reflection about process and product. Use criteria of choice for the rubric that includes some or all of the following questions.

Pre-search

- Has the student chosen a personally meaningful topic?
- Does the topic involve decision-making and problem-solving?
- Does the student display an ability to use a number of strategies to choose a topic—i.e., webbing, index searching, general reading, and interviewing parents and people who know him/her?
- Does the student understand the topic's limitations and is the student willing to change topics if necessary?
- Can the student create original search questions that move

beyond facts and that facilitate solving the problem or making the decision?

- Can the student demonstrate use of information tools, such as electronic indexes and tables of contents, to choose key words that lead to open-ended search questions?
- Can the student focus his/her topic on a reasonable number of related questions?
- Does the student show organizational strengths through an ability to prioritize potential topics, search questions, resource choices, and alternative solutions?

Search

- Has the student looked at a sufficient variety of sources or interview appropriate contacts/experts in the content area?
- Has the student demonstrated strong information literacy skills in locating, assessing, and using sources?
- Does the student demonstrate an ability to discard irrelevant sources, as evidenced through learning log notes and bibliography?
- Does the student demonstrate use of an organizing technique for notetaking, such as double-entry drafting, highlighting, and marginal notes?
- Does the learning log show evidence of adequate reflection on double-entry draft entries?
- Does the student show an organized approach to solving the problem or making the decision?
- Does the student apply information from a variety of sources for solving the problem or making the decision?

Presentation

- Has the student actually followed through on what the student wanted to accomplish through the search questions?
- Does the student present a clear and well-supported paper or presentation?
- Can the student articulate a personal search strategy to be used in a future assignment?
- Does the paper or presentation reveal clear evidence of effort by the student to carry through the strategies taught through the unit?
- Are the conclusions in the paper or presentation based on information gathered from multiple sources?

Writing

One of the strengths of the I-Search is the first-person narrative natural language. Students write naturally about a topic of concern to themselves. Consider the natural flow of the student's language as the most critical factor.

- Does the product demonstrate strong topic development?
- Does the product demonstrate an ability of the student to express thoughts in the first person?
- Does the product present content in a focused, clear, and logical order?
- Does the product provide examples which develop the main points?
- Are the sentences in the final product complete and correct, varied in structure and length?
- Does the student use appropriate vocabulary?
- Does the student use good spelling, capitalization, punctuation, and paragraphing?

Each of these questions derives from experience with students who skipped some of the process steps. The skippers had the most difficulty completing the assignment satisfactorily. As a result, they did not add some of the most important strategies to their personal research process. This, in turn, resulted in poor quality transference of process and strategies to other problems or assignments.

These questions scaffold the development of a rubric for students to assess themselves, balanced by your assessment. Or, with your guidance, let students create their own criteria for judging certain aspects of the process. The more you involve students with assessment, the more pride students take in the quality of their I-Search.

Finally, ask students to reflect on the I-Search unit itself. Their responses should underscore the power of the I-Search process. Their responses will certainly indicate where the unit needs improvement and identify the most effective strategies.

> Involving students in self-assessment produces more pride in their products.

REFERENCES

Redding, N. (1994). "Assessing the big outcomes." In Kuhlthau, C. C. (ed.). *Assessment and the school library media center.* (pp. 131–136). Englewood, CO: Libraries Unlimited.

Macrorie, K. (1988). *The I-Search paper*. Rev. ed. Portsmouth, NH: Heinemann.

Stripling, B. K. (1995). Learning-centered libraries: Implications from research. *School Library Media Quarterly, 23*(3), pp. 163–170.

Part II
I-Search Connections

7 DEVELOPING I-SEARCH MANAGEMENT STRATEGIES

Management is critical to the success of the I-Search because of the options for partial or complete I-Searches, either in a curriculum content area or by itself as an independent topic choice research unit. Some units end within a very short time frame while other units continue for a six-week period. Depending on unit learning goals, teachers and media specialists guide students in their task management and progress assessment as part of student scaffolding.

> Task management and process assessment are vital parts of the I-Search.

Conferences and responses to learning log reflections support the process. Evaluation and assessment at critical points during the unit ensure good research practice. Students who do not fully invest in their topic tend to skip steps and revert to previous practices and patterns of behavior during research projects. Their problems with process are the direct result of their neglect of steps until the last minute. The strongest antidote is assessing their reflections on the strategies and process in their learning logs throughout the assignment. Observe how they use the strategies and to what degree of completeness. If they write a negative reflection about a strategy's strength and weakness, respect it and support them in choosing an alternative strategy to accomplish what they need to do.

Track students closely from step to step by using a checklist and/or a formative assessment rubric to ascertain student success at each stage. Otherwise, some students take advantage of the freedoms provided by the I-Search to revert to past unsatisfactory practices, such as cutting and pasting information into minimum source papers written overnight. The students who find it difficult to write in the first person should respond to question probes to get them started. If they revert to old practices, their papers frequently become a composite of facts put together in typical fashion without the construction of new ideas or applications. They do not take ownership of their content if the questions are not their own. Rather, they compile factual information to satisfy what they think the teaching team wants for the assignment. Once off track, it is almost impossible for students working without help to use information and their own critical thinking to answer their essential question for themselves, not the reader.

Two specific goals are valuable to keep in mind:

- Provide adequate time for students to move through the process.
- Create an atmosphere of cooperation to facilitate success.

Students need time to move through the process.
Cooperation facilitates success.

UNIT TIMELINE SUGGESTIONS

Suggesting a timeline is always a problem with the I-Search. Learning goals and the curriculum schedule will dictate how much time and energy the teaching team has to offer students. The level of student information research skills and understanding of the research process will dictate the length of the I-Search. If the objective is to tweak their knowledge of research strategies via a curriculum unit assignment, then individual strategies from the I-Search process might be enough. If students are starting from the beginning with development of their individual research processes or have an ingrained, ineffective research process, a more complete I-Search assignment would be beneficial. The full I-Search is an excellent tool for creating a foundation for using other research processes, more formal in their requirements. After an I-Search unit is completed, give students another research project in a curriculum area and observe the difference in the way they approach it. Most of them will integrate the strategies that provide the most success during the I-Search. They will not need to ask how to start their project. They use their increased research competence to produce higher-caliber products. The I-Search has so much flexibility for a variety of research needs. Knowledge of students' information literacy skills and problem-solving needs is the critical tool for deciding which strategies to integrate or how much of an I-Search to attempt.

Integrating one or more of the strategies into content area units would not take as much time and is useful as a substitute for building student information literacy skills incrementally. In this era of criterion reference testing on a national level, e.g., skills and competencies, teachers can integrate the individual strategies within a series of mini-research units and still achieve their research goal. In such cases, the amount of time spent depends on the number of steps you want to include. It might also depend on the type of assignment, the content area, or the grade level of the students. A critical component is reflective time on the topic, process, and information synthesis for the final product.

If time prohibits a full I-Search unit, integrate one or more strategies into content units with research assignments.

The following timeline can serve as a possible model for a full I-Search unit. If you begin the I-Search unit the week before Thanksgiving break, students can complete the webbing exercise in time to discuss their web with family members, relatives, and friends during the holiday. Between the Thanksgiving and Christmas holidays, students gather, find, and apply information. They keep detailed records of their actions, thoughts, and feelings in their learning logs. The Christmas holiday gives students time to reflect on the information they gather and process. Sometimes, it is a time for distancing and gaining a fresh perspective on the material. Upon return to school in January, they:

- refine their essential topic questions through the pre-notetaking strategy;
- use the double-entry drafts to gather information with their reflections on how that information informs their essential questions;
- reflect about their findings and strategies in their learning logs; and
- complete a final product.

Scheduling I-Search units at the end of the school year produces mixed results. While students appreciate the hands-on learning experiences—i.e., working with information technology, sharing with other students, and conducting interviews associated with the I-Search—the impending end of the school year induces them to think more about summer vacation than school. They tend to spend less energy absorbing what the I-Search has to offer. On the other hand, participating in an I-Search unit after taking a battery of state and national examinations might be a refreshing change and keep the students' minds active and alert during the remaining school days.

INDIVIDUALIZED STUDENT TIMELINES

When you establish tentative deadlines at various stages of the process, you ensure that students stay within the unit's time frame. The I-Search requires more individual student responsibility than most students have experienced; thus, they may need support, such as checklists and calendars that help them with that responsibility.

Each student moves through the process at a slightly different rate. Dana's story is an example. After introduction to the I-Search unit, she discovered that she would be absent for the next two days. Dana would miss the webbing activity leading to topic selection. Her parents want her to attend a private school the next year, and she will visit several schools. Her parents are leaving the decision up to her about which school to attend. In Dana's case, this seems a natural I-Search question. The teaching team decides to give her an altered timeline. Instead of spending time

> Creating a personalized checklist of activities to complete is a strong organization intervention.

on a personal interest web, she moves straight to a school's web where she identifies criteria that are important to her and the specific interests she wants to investigate. From the school's web, she moves into the pre-notetaking phase, producing a list of questions to ask while visiting private schools. Before she returned to school, Dana wrote a narrative of her visit in her learning log and created double-entry drafts for each school visit and her interviews, noting in the left column all the major pros and cons about each school, and in the right column her reactions to the pros and cons.

When students encounter temporary obstacles, you can adapt their schedules to their needs, while fitting them to your overall timeline. Because of frequent conferencing within the process, you can support students in this way. One of the most common situations is the student who must change topics for whatever reason, be it lack of interest after finishing the preliminary essential question-making, or discovery of a more motivating essential question. Return the student to his/her personal interest web and ask him/her to select another topic. The student completes a first draft of the pre-notetaking sheet, does some general background reading, and then develops a second draft of the pre-notetaking sheet with the higher-order essential question and subquestions. Extend the deadline for completing the new pre-notetaking sheet, but advise the student to work harder to catch up to the rest of the class.

DEBRIEFING

The timeline provides an overview of the process, steps and activities, and sets potential deadlines. However, flexibility should characterize the teaching team's attitude toward time, if possible. You might want to modify the I-Search timeline based on input you are receiving from conferencing and debriefing with students. Student input through class sharing and learning logs will tell you where the students are in the process, what obstacles they are encountering, and what aspects of the search they find confusing. How you scaffold certain student skills or behaviors through interventions before students move to the next step will be important to their success and lessen feelings of anxiety or frustration. Moving too fast might inhibit their use of each strategy. If necessary, you can provide more practice in the use of a specific strategy or seek out an alternative activity.

Make it a point to debrief students after modeling each strategy or technique to let you know if students understand what they need to do. After the lesson on double-entry drafting, for example, brainstorm with students what they like or dislike about double-entry drafting. Find out how this strategy helps them generate ideas for their learning logs. Sharing reactions and understandings about each strategy reinforces the value of a technique.

Listening to students is a critical technique for assessing the I-Search process. It allows you to make necessary modifications and overcome potential obstacles before they become permanent barriers. When the process is moving smoothly, debriefing sessions give students reassurance that they are progressing in the right direction.

> Debrief students after modeling a new strategy to assess how much they understand.

INTERVENTIONS

Interventions fall into two categories: full-group interventions devoted to content assessment, and individualized interventions that serve a variety of purposes. Group conferencing when several students need help reinforces the strategy for other students. Most interventions will occur during topic choice, question-making, reflective responses, and the transition from learning log to the final product.

During webbing, the teaching team meets with all students to discuss their topics and brainstorm various aspects of the topics. Is the topic truly choosing them? Or, for the sake of having a topic, are they picking the first subject that seems attractive? Is their lack of experience with analysis causing them to miss possible topics from their interest web? Does the web need more information before they make a selection? To encourage students, have them generate more ideas and select a personally meaningful subject through class brainstorming.

In the case of pre-notetaking and double-entry drafting, the intervention is designed to move all students from lower levels on Bloom's *Taxonomy* into upper-level critical thinking and to provide reassurance. During pre-notetaking conferences, the teaching team assists students in developing challenging research questions. Where do their questions fall on the taxonomy? How can they move to a higher level of critical thinking? How can you help them identify the one or two essential questions for their search, under which they can organize their other questions? Guide them by having them rephrase their essential questions, wherever possible, into *how, why,* and/or *which* questions that ask for process, explanations, and comparisons or contrasts.

During double-entry drafting, you intervene through conferencing or by writing comments on students' double-entry drafts or in their learning logs. Have them respond to your comments with their own reflections on what they are doing. Reflective thinking is difficult for many students in an academic environment, because of the lecture/test methods in general use.

Individual student interventions involve helping a student develop study skills which match a student's personal learning style, and assisting a student in finding resources unique to the chosen topic. Early in the process, identify the students who need help with organization and sequencing, as evident through their learning log reflections. A learning log might reveal that a student is weak in reflective thinking. While other students are working on double-entry drafts, this student might be trying to decide what information to highlight in his/her articles. One remedy is to give the student a checklist of activities to follow in order to create a successful double-entry draft. If the student still does not make progress with reflective notetaking skills, a further conference might reveal an additional problem, such as trying to make the strategy too complicated.

Jack does not feign ignorance to avoid work. He cannot make the connection between research questions and reading for information. Jack also makes a false assumption: If he finds an activity easy, he must be doing something wrong. A conference quickly resolves his misconceptions, and the next day, Jack presents his highlighted articles. His previous problems also indicate that another intervention on creating double-entry drafts might be in order before moving to the next step.

Some students have organizational problems. An intervention with one of these students could result in creation of a personalized checklist of activities. When students feel overwhelmed by the steps in the process, they hesitate, and their fear of failure becomes an obstacle in itself. It is somewhat like having a multitude of resources placed in front of them. They do not know what to do with all the information; much less, have they formed a focus for their research. This is a common occurrence in the traditional school research paper. There's no place to start, and some students would rather not try than fail in the doing. Thus, they copy and paste the factual material or others' opinions and call it their own work. To overcome this problem in severe cases, a daily intervention might result in individualized lesson plans. Meet with these students at the beginning of the period to determine one specific goal to complete by the end of the period. Near the end

> Identify students who need help with organization and sequencing as early in the process as possible.

of the period, check their progress. Help them design a homework assignment that will move them through the next step. Breaking the process into small steps helps these students feel less intimidated. Combine this strategy with reassurance and praise for each accomplishment to help students who feel threatened by the process.

Some intervention involves matching activities with learning styles. Mike is a hands-on and auditory learner who wants to learn about underwater welding for his career. A video on welding gives him background information on his subject. He also uses a computer program in the media center to obtain a printout of technical colleges offering training in underwater welding. These sources help Mike create questions for an interview with the welding instructor. He records the interview with the instructor's approval. After the interview, Mike listens to the tape and finds passages he wants to add to his double-entry drafts. They tell him what he needs to know to complete the school's welding course. His resource investigation and reflection strategies match his learning style.

Interventions have many purposes and take many formats. They require class time, planning, and management strategies.

HOMEWORK

Although class time facilitates individualized work on the I-Search process, homework is still a necessary component of the process. It is essential for adequate reflection throughout the process. At home, students talk with parents, guardians, close relatives, and/or adult friends about their webbing diagrams and topic selection. During the pre-notetaking stage, students bring home computer printouts and photocopies of articles so that they can skim them and create questions. They find Web sites to investigate. Students evaluate and create double-entry drafts for the Web sites and other resources, and plan and conduct interviews. Students fill in their double-entry drafts at home and then write learning log entries.

A common homework activity is reflecting on the day's class work. What are their actions, feelings, and thoughts for the day? Check on students' use of time at home during conferences by asking them to show their work or describe how they are using their time outside of class.

Check on students' use of homework time by asking them to show you what they have accomplished during your conferences.

Take a curriculum break during the I-Search to give students a time to reflect.

TAKE A BREAK

I-Search units can be intense and require a commitment of time and energy, shared by media specialists and teachers who collaborate on a unit plan and debrief before and after classes. During class, you meet individually with students, giving them support to select personally meaningful topics, which often have an emotional aspect as well. When students want to deal with topics such as divorce, adoption, illness, and death, they must have parental permission and support, and, frequently, involvement.

At times during the I-Search unit, you and the students will feel overwhelmed. This is the time for a break. While students are gathering or processing information outside of school, use class time to start other curriculum units, or design several one- or two-day curriculum activities into the time frame. Not only does this provide a break for students dealing with emotional issues, but it also provides "catch up" time.

Clearly, the full I-Search can be time-consuming if students have little or no experience with I-Searching and need to start fresh with introductory training in each strategy. Assigning an I-Search project in another unit will reinforce their process skills and confidence. Or if time is a barrier and constraint, as it is with many teachers faced with state and national exams for their students, downsize the unit according to learning goals, curriculum unit needs, and time available. In spite of such downsizing, the strategies used in the I-Search have much to offer individually for strengthening student research skills.

COOPERATIVE LEARNING AND TRAINING FOR PEER EDITING

Group activity facilitates the sharing of content and process for I-Searching. To promote peer teaching, mix students with different strengths and abilities. For example, place a student who is good at generating details in a group with a student who has excellent organizational stills. A third student in the group may be skillful at spotting logical and illogical arguments, while a fourth is a natural leader. In short, each student complements the others. At various stages of the process, have students meet with the members of their groups. Students take turns reading excerpts from their learning logs, or, at the end of the unit, drafts of their I-Search papers. When each reading is completed, listeners in the group comment on the contents.

Following Macrorie's (1988) suggestions for peer editing, which emphasize a nonthreatening atmosphere, train students to ask questions to alert the authors about problems. The following are question starters for the peer editors that address issues of content and process:

Prepare peer editors by giving them content and process probes to help them edit helpfully.

Content Questions

1. I am confused by ———. Can you explain it to me?
2. What other details support ———?
3. Can you think of another way of arranging your key points?
4. What is the main idea?
5. What are the opposing viewpoints to your opinion?

Process Questions

1. How will you find more information? What other resources might you consult?
2. What problem do you face here? How will you overcome it? Have you tried ———?
3. How current is this material?
4. Why might the author be biased?
5. What is your next step?

Using questions instead of making critical comments helps maintain a positive atmosphere and encourage student writers to explore possibilities. Ownership of the writing stays with the authors who can choose to accept or ignore the suggestions.

Use a "fly on the wall" approach to facilitate sharing groups. Move from group to group listening to discussions and intervening when necessary. Interventions include keeping students on task by reminding them of the group's purpose or procedures, encouraging a quiet or shy student to ask a question, and reminding students who dominate the discussion to share their time with others.

SHARE RESPONSIBILITIES

> One of the I-Search's strongest assets is its appropriateness for collaborative planning and teaching.

The I-Search, presents an excellent opportunity to practice collaborative planning and teaching. It provides a natural opening for the media specialist and teacher to plan a unit together, designing both content and information literacy objectives, planning activities, sharing teaching, assessing student learning, and evaluating the unit jointly.

At first, more responsibilities are placed on the partner who is adept at process teaching. Gradually, as the other partner gains understanding of the process approach, he or she will share responsibilities. The demands of sharing also depend on the depth of the unit conducted. If the I-Search is used for a short activity, one person is generally capable of handling the teaching and assessment. An extended unit requires both being available. Class size is an important consideration. Student topic choice I-Searches or content area I-Search research projects also make a difference in the teaching responsibilities.

> Collaborative partners negotiate planning and teaching responsibilities.

A frequent question asked at I-Search training workshops involves division of labor. How do the media specialist and classroom teaching partner share responsibilities? If both work as a team to design these units, each has an opportunity to contribute expertise—the classroom teacher in the content area and the media specialist with information literacy skills. Both will model the webbing activity with one partner questioning the person being interviewed and the other recording the responses. Then you use a similar model for the pre-notetaking demonstration. For example, the media specialist gives a lesson on how to use key words to write research questions. The teacher has the class brainstorm questions for a sample topic from the content area. The media specialist records the student responses on the computerized smart board. Together, you conduct a follow-up discussion on how to evaluate the questions for critical thinking at the upper level of Bloom's hierarchy. As a result of this sharing of labor, students perceive teacher and media specialist as a team with equal authority. This establishes the atmosphere for sharing other responsibilities such as conferencing and assessment.

Both media specialist and teacher should try to meet periodically with each student. This requires coordination so that individual students do not receive conflicting messages. Together, you review your conferences and give each other a brief assessment of student progress. Debriefing time is for sharing and problem-solving, with joint planning helping to solidify the partnership.

Sharing creates a chemistry which facilitates new ideas for unit instruction. If the classes are large, you can meet with students in small groups listening to comments on the students' research process. You can contribute ideas for additional resources or, perhaps, questions that facilitate a different perspective on the research.

Not all partnerships involve an equal division of labor, particularly when one person initiates the I-Search. Part of it depends on the process advocate. One scenario might have the teacher taking more responsibility for the I-Search with the media specialist concentrating on information skills and resource acquisition. Or, at other times, the media specialist becomes the catalyst for change and promotes the I-Search to the teacher.

At times, media specialists will shy away from suggesting more work for the teacher through the I-Search. At other times, the teacher will be reluctant to approach the busy media specialist to ask for assistance with the I-Search. But once this barrier is broken and both see the improved learning of students, neither will be shy to repeat the I-Search together. All it takes is one time and a willing teacher and media specialist to be pioneers in your school.

PERSONALIZE THE PROCESS

Ultimately, each student's I-Search is unique to his or her personal experience. The same is true for media specialists and teachers who develop their own strategies and techniques that apply to your environment. Personalize the process to match student needs with the ingredients that work best. Experience should be the model.

Learning how to teach the I-Search is a process in itself. The first time through will seem awkward in comparison with the ease of assigning a research topic and then turning the students loose. However, notice the difference in student learning growth and student products, and any mistakes and problems will seem minor compared to the enthusiasm of most students. From the beginning, involve students in the learning process with the I-Search. Encourage them to contribute ideas, suggestions, and evaluate what worked and what did not. Not only will they take ownership of their I-Search but ownership of the unit as well.

Students will appreciate participating in the decision-making process and knowing that their opinions count. They will value

Students will willingly share input on what worked and what needs improvement in the I-Search unit.

recounting their experiences and what they learned; it will make them feel important and increase their success in understanding their own research process. Giving students a vested interest in the process as well as the product can have a ripple effect on their lives.

8 LINKING I-SEARCH AND CURRICULUM CONTENT AREAS

The I-Search process works well as a research process in the content areas.

Students need enough background information to choose an interesting topic.

The I-Search is a powerful research process for content area topics; the strategies are almost the same as for student-selected topics. The basic difference is that students choose their topics within the content area, using tools specifically for a content area I-Search. They must have enough background knowledge to brainstorm a number of interesting topics that they would like to explore. A great strategy for boosting content area knowledge for high school students is the "book share" strategy.

The library media specialist and partner teacher select a variety of books related to the general topic (e.g., the Civil War, heredity, the U.S. Constitution, presidential elections, atoms, etc.). Choose books that are general in nature, such as subject area encyclopedias and others that focus on a section of the general topic. Students then choose a book to "share" with classmates after you model the process they will complete.

Figure 8.1.   Template: Book Share Worksheet

Book Share Template

Name: Course:

Date: Teacher:

Book Share

Author _____

Title _____

Directions: Skim the cover or book jacket, inside blurbs, and preface, introduction, and end pages for the content ideas. Record the information below. Then prepare a two-minute book share that answers the following question: What did you learn about the book that might encourage others to read it? What topics are covered in the book?

To prepare for the presentation, answer the following questions:

   1. What is the focus of this book?

   2. How is information organized in the table of contents?

   3. Speculate on the author's point of view and the author's approach to the subject based on the table of contents, preface, and/or dust jacket.

   4. What types of graphics (e.g., charts, graphs, maps, photographs, flowcharts, diagrams, etc.) will the reader find in this book?

   5. What is the author's background?

   6. Based on your review, list three potential research topics.

The media specialist chooses one of the books, reviews the contents with the students, and then models how he/she will complete the Book Share form (Figure 8.1). After modeling the book, ask each student to select one of the books, complete the Book Share form, and share his or her findings with the class. While listening to other students' book shares, each student keeps a list of titles and authors and records two or three interesting facts about each book so that he/she can remember its contents. The student puts a check in front of books he/she might select to read. When students complete their Book Share forms, you compile the list of potential topics on a large piece of paper and post the paper in a convenient spot in the library media center. When more than one class is working on the same content area, encourage the students to compare the lists.

Students spend two sessions over a few days' time in the library media center, reading chapters and/or pieces from the books they share or finding other materials in the library media center on the content area topics that intrigue them. The more parts of the content area that arouse their curiosity, the closer they are to finding an engaging topic. At the end of each class period, students spend five minutes writing a learning log entry summarizing their reading and suggesting potential research questions. By the end of the two days in the media center, students usually have a focus for their content area research. You can tell by what they write in their logs.

> Students need sufficient content area background knowledge to create reasonable, higher-order questions that interest them.

When students have sufficient content area background knowledge to create reasonable, higher-order questions, ask them to draw a web of their interest choice in the content area, using as the focus their anticipated research question. Ask them to expand the idea on their web as much as their current knowledge permits. Then try the accordion exercise with the class, as described in Chapter 4, with each student preparing a sheet for the topic they think is the most interesting. At the top of the folded sheet, the student notes the topic, but not in a question format. As the sheet circulates around the class, the others write questions about the topic that they would like to see the student research. These questions serve as probes to get the topic initiator thinking about what interests him/her most about the topic.

Creating the first pre-notetaking sheet draft comes next, with students noting what they know about the topic, what they don't know, and what they would like to know about the topic. Other students' questions boost the ability to recognize what they do not know, as well as pique interest and help them focus on what they would like to know.

Once students succeed with these steps, the rest of the I-Search strategies previously introduced help them complete their quest. They complete additional background reading beyond the book sharing in the general topic interest area and reflect in their learning logs about what they want to know, based on background reading. Then they draft a second pre-notetaking sheet that narrows focus questions and translates them into a higher-order format. They proceed to the double-entry drafts for taking notes from resources and respond to those notes reflectively as they locate information that informs their questions. They write reflections about these responses in their learning logs, and conference with you to keep them on track and support their search. At any point in time, they revisit previous steps to change focus and questions according to their new needs and interests, based on what they are finding. The process is iterative, giving students the same opportunity as they have outside of school to acknowledge that their research process informs their perspectives and opinions and, sometimes, produces changes.

When the curriculum teaching schedule does not permit a complete content area I-Search, teachers may still want students to polish their research skills with a modified research project. Design a project that incorporates learning needs for students, as well as acknowledges their current level of research process sophistication. When using one or more of the I-Search strategies, but not a complete I-Search process, you should first investigate student skill levels with research. A survey of students' past research experiences and familiar research techniques identifies what additional skills and strategies they need to move their research experience to a higher level of challenge and critical thinking quality, as well as produce a product that promotes learning growth.

RESEARCH SURVEY QUESTIONS

Use the following questions to identify where students are in their knowledge of the research process:

1. When you last completed a research project in one of your courses, did you get to choose the topic or did the teacher assign it?
2. If you chose the topic, describe how you chose it.
3. Were you asked to create and answer a specific question about your topic or were you given the topic and asked to find out information about it?

4. Where did you find most of your information? Media center materials———, parents, friends———, community experts———, Internet———
5. How did you decide when the information you found was accurate?
6. How did you decide when you had enough information to complete your research?
7. Did you conference with your teacher during your research to talk about what you were doing in your research?
8. Were you asked to reflect on what you found, how you found it, and how important it was for what you were going to write about your topic?
9. Did you keep a learning log or journal with reflections about your search and topic?
10. Do you have the technology skills to turn in a computer word processed paper or create a PowerPoint about your topic?
11. When you get a research assignment, what steps do you take to begin it?
12. What do you think about when you hear the term "research"?

This list is not complete but should help identify what students have done and what research skills and understandings they have. For example, if they have never been asked to create a research question from a topic assignment, spend time on the prenotetaking strategy to help with question identification and format. If they have thought reflectively about their topics as they search for information, it would be appropriate to introduce double-entry drafting and learning logs. The objective is to add just enough effective strategies to their repertoire of research skills to increase their effectiveness and critical thinking in the research process.

COLLABORATION AMONG TEACHERS AND MEDIA SPECIALISTS

> One of the I-Search's strongest assets is its appropriateness for collaborative planning and teaching.

The I-Search, whether complete or partial, is an excellent format for initiating collaborative partnerships within the curriculum. By working together, you can offer students more types of scaffolding and process expertise. You share the unit planning with your partner to generate more ideas for teaching and learning. The classroom teacher knows the students and the curriculum content goals; the media specialist knows the kinds of information literacy, information technology, and research strategies (e.g., the I-Search) necessary for student learning success. If application technologies are involved and students do not have adequate skills, the technology specialist helps in that area. Together, you incorporate information literacy and technology literacy skills with content learning. Together, unpack the professional standards for the content area, information literacy, and technology literacy to guide development of learning goals, integrate them in the teaching and learning activities, and assess student achievement and learning at formative and summative stages in the unit. Together, evaluate what works and what needs improvement for the next time.

All partners should keep a record of the unit plans, the teacher in her planning book, the media specialist in a curriculum unit database, the technology specialist in a database or planning book, as well as the resources, the strategies, the responsibilities of each, and student assignments. Note on the records the improvements you need to make for the next time, as a result of the unit evaluation. The media specialist adds the unit to the school's curriculum map, which displays what actually is taught by whom and how (not what is prescribed). The media specialist can then prepare to participate in any new planning necessary for the unit and have the new resources ready as necessary. Next, you identify any additional standards that can be integrated into the unit and analyze what technologies enhance teaching and student learning. Decide together what kinds of skills students must have to use the information and application technologies successfully. If skills need to be introduced or reinforced, decide how to teach the skills to students.

> Collaborative partners negotiate planning and teaching responsibilities.

> Note on the plan records the improvements necessary for the next time you teach the unit.

COLLABORATIVE PLANNING TOOLS

A collaborative planning worksheet template is an excellent tool to use to plan. The media specialist can use the template to take notes for later entry into the database for collaborative units. The sheet will have items for essential information, goals, participant responsibilities, resources, and technologies. If a template is used, make the planning information available in a database or other available format in the media center for people to use and add their own suggestions. When the unit is a building block for additional learning growth later, the team that plans collaboratively the next level unit will know what students learned in this unit.

The University of Georgia students use an effective collaborative planning worksheet template (Figure 8.2). It contains space for the essential pieces of the unit plan, not the individual lesson plans. It has a place to indicate the literacy strategies to introduce, as well as the student skill levels essential for success. You can adapt the collaborative planning template for your use by adjusting the categories to fit your goals. Feel free to do so. Even if the unit is not planned collaboratively, the template records essential information for curriculum mapping and the next time teaching the unit.

A planning worksheet is an invaluable tool for collaborative planning.

Figure 8.2.   Template: Collaborative Planning Worksheet

**Collaborative Planning Worksheet Template
(Developed by University of Georgia Students)**

Teacher Name: _____   Grade Level: _____

Title of Unit: _____

Date Taught: _____   Length of Unit: _____

Subjects Addressed:

Unit Goals:

QCCs or other objectives:

Teaching Pedagogies:
___lecture
___independent work
___demonstration
___games
___learning centers
___discussion
___research
___discovery
___other:

Class Organization:
___whole class
___small groups
___collaborative pairs
___individual

Information Literacies: (based on *Information Power, pages 8–9*)
___accessing information efficiently and effectively
___evaluating information critically and competently
___using information accurately and creatively
___pursuing information related to topics of personal interest

---

Figure 8.2. *(Continued)*

___appreciating of literature and creative expression
___striving for excellence in information seeking and knowledge
___recognizing the importance of information in a democratic society
___practicing ethical behavior regarding information
___participating effectively in groups to pursue and generate information

Technology Literacies: (based on QCCs)
___utilizes technology to facilitate writing process
___utilizes technology to create charts and graphs
___uses multimedia tools to express ideas
___uses brainstorming/webbing software in planning, organizing, and pre-writing
___uses basic research techniques with teacher guidance
___other:

Research Strategies: (based on I-Search)
___creating an interest map, brainstorming for key words and terms
___identifying and researching a topic of personal interest
___listing what is already known about topic and what one wants to know
___creating higher-order questions
___general reading
___locating appropriate sources of information
___double-entry drafting
___developing interview skills
___evaluating information for usefulness and accuracy
___creating a product of a search for information
___using information to answer research questions
___peer editing
___reflecting on success of research process

Classroom Teacher Instructional Responsibilities:

Media Specialist Responsibilities:

Resources Needed:

Figure 8.2. *(Continued)*

Unit Title: _____

Teacher: _____

Date: _____

Post-Unit Evaluation Questions
(for Classroom Teacher and Media Specialist)

What was the most successful aspect of the unit in terms of:

information literacy:

subject area content:

student enjoyment and motivation:

What was the least successful aspect of the unit in terms of:

information literacy:

subject area content:

student enjoyment and motivation:

Which resources were the most useful?

Which resources should be reconsidered?

What additional materials could be acquired to improve this unit?

What teaching strategies should be considered or reviewed for next year?

What were the biggest surprises or pitfalls in this unit?

Is more scaffolding for students needed in any area?

Are there any strategies or teaching methods used in this unit that could be applied elsewhere across the curriculum?

Additional Thoughts:

CURRICULUM MAP AS A COLLABORATIVE PLANNING TOOL

Eisenberg and Berkowitz (1988) developed a curriculum mapping technique that records units as they are actually taught, not what should be taught. This type of map is a graphic that indicates the major content area units taught during the year by each grade level or discipline area teacher. It is not a curriculum guide telling the teacher what he should teach. Rather, it is a graphic of what the teacher actually teaches: how and when. Each teacher completes a unit template for the major units he teaches during the year. These units may transcend disciplines, require outside resources, utilize information literacy and technology skills, and lend themselves to collaborative partnerships. These are units that integrate the major curriculum standards for the content areas or serve as knowledge builders for units in succeeding grades, such as animals, the solar system, World War II, electricity, authors of the Twentieth Century, careers, diseases and the body, etc. Most likely, these units will consist of multiple lesson plans.

When the media specialist creates a map of these units and posts it on the media center's wall, teachers see at a glance what others are teaching at the same time and what's next. Media specialists and teachers analyze the map for which units:

> A curriculum map of what is being taught, not what should be taught, will help identify where the teacher needs additional support for the unit.

- lend themselves to information literacy skills integration, such as the I-Search offers;
- invite an interdisciplinary approach and collaborative planning;
- use media center or special resources outside of the textbook;
- require additional resources to be included in the following year's budget;
- require reservations for class time in the media center;
- include research projects;
- take a constructive approach to learning;
- make use of authentic assessments;
- require technologies and software; and/or
- duplicate another teacher's efforts with the same students or a unit at a different grade level.

By looking at the content area units, you can identify the units that include research assignments that might lend themselves to I-Search strategies that will enhance student learning. The cur-

The curriculum map should indicate which units are resource-based and have assessments requiring information literacy and/or technology literacy skills.

riculum map information template (Figure 8.3) suggests the kinds of information valuable for curriculum mapping.

While most of the template information would be kept in a curriculum map database and/or notebook available for all to use, the map should indicate enough unit information to know how much involvement the library media center would have, such as name, grade, content area, name of unit, date taught, collaborative planning partners, assessment product (test, report, etc.), resource or textbook based, media center time reserved, technology used, and information literacy skills taught. Don't hesitate to adapt the curriculum map information template to individual teacher needs. Notice that many items on the curriculum map information template are similar to the collaborative planning worksheet template.

Figure 8.3. Template: Curriculum Map Information Worksheet

Curriculum Map Information Template
(Developed by University of Georgia students)

Teacher:

Grade:

Subject Area:

Unit:

Dates Taught:

Name of textbook used (if none, state "none"):

Unit goal(s):

Research unit: yes_____ no_____

Content area learning goals:

Curriculum standards met:

Information literacy standards met:

Technology standards met:

Figure 8.3.   (*Continued*)

Resources:

    Textbook only_____

    Textbook with supplemental resources_____

Resources with no textbook_____

Primary teaching method:

Classroom teacher responsibilities:

Media specialist responsibilities:

Technology specialist responsibilities:

Student assessment products:

Technologies used:

CURRICULUM UNITS THAT INTEGRATE I-SEARCH STRATEGIES

There are two ways to analyze units that could be enhanced with the addition of I-Search strategies:

- Look at the units as they have been taught in previous years to evaluate whether research process skills would strengthen student learning growth and fulfill content goals; and
- Plan a new curriculum content unit from the beginning with learning goals that lend themselves to research.

Choose individual I-Search strategies to enhance learning growth in non-I-Search units.

Figure 8.4 summarizes a high school content area unit that one in-service teacher designed to include I-Search strategies. An analysis of how the I-Search strategies strengthen the learning goals follows the unit. Note that the unit write-up is in the format of an adapted collaborative planning template.

Figure 8.4.   Sample: Georgia Counties Collaborative Project

Georgia Counties Collaborative Project
(an example using the I-Search pre-search strategies)

Designed by Kathy Traylor and Colleagues

Collaborators:
Kathy Traylor, 8th grade algebra teacher
8th grade social studies teacher(s)
Media specialists, media clerk
Technology specialist

County Curriculum Standards:
Algebra 1
    Learn to communicate mathematically
    Become mathematical problem solvers
    Learn to use mathematics in their daily lives
    Learn to reason mathematically
    A – Algebra (8MAA_A2003-1, 2, 4, 5, 7, 9, 10, 11, 17, 20, 21, 22)
    C – Computation and Estimation (8MAA_C2003–30 through –32)
    F – Statistics (8MAA_F2003–40 through –44)
Social Studies
    A – Map and Globe Skills (8SS_A1998-3 through 6)
    B – Information Processing Skills (8SS_B1998-7 through 13, 18, 19)
    G – 20th Century Transformation (8SS_G200-13 through 16)

Topic: Georgia's Counties

Subjects: 8th grade algebra and 8th grade social studies (Georgia and U.S. history and geography)

Duration: This will be an ongoing project throughout the year.

Instructional Organization: Whole class, Collaborative Pairs, Small group, and Individuals, at various times during the project

Teaching Pedagogies: Demonstration, Independent work, Research, Project-based Learning

Student Assessment: Assessment will primarily be by rubrics, but will vary according to the specific assignment.

Research Skills and Strategies

1. After an introduction to Georgia's county system and examination of the county map in the social studies textbook, use webbing to determine what Georgia county might interest you. Your web might include places you or your relatives have lived or visited, names that interest

Figure 8.4. (*Continued*)

you [I had a student select "Bacon" and "Coffee" counties because she liked that combination of names. This will be a homework assignment so students can ask relevant questions at home]. Then select a county to study.

2. General information: Students will read the general information About Georgia's Counties (http://www.cviog.uga.edu/Projects/gainfo/countyhistory.htm)

3. Create a three-column pre-notetaking sheet listing what you know about that county, what you don't know, and what you'd like to know. Keep in mind that you will need to be creating graphs and charts from this information. [In-class lesson will model this using our county as an example, which will provide students with some ideas as to the types of information to look for].

4. Turn the pre-notes into questions. Form several research questions based on the pre-notetaking. Include 'compare and contrast' questions. You can compare and contrast your county of choice to our county, or compare and contrast two different time periods in your county.

5. For each math assignment, select a research question that you can answer with that math assignment. For example, if the math assignment asks you to create a circle (pie) graph, you might choose a research question about the racial makeup or educational levels of the county's residents.

6. Locate information – Media specialist, in collaboration with math and social studies teachers, will create a "pathfinder" sheet with starting points such as the Georgia Counties Web site, created by UGA's Carl Vinson Institute of Government. (http://www.cviog.uga.edu/Projects/gainfo/county.htm) [Students could complete this whole project using only the links from this Web site!]

7. Evaluate information for usefulness. Determine if it will answer your research question and then answer the question.

8. Evaluate success of research process

Information Literacy Skills

1. Access information efficiently and effectively: Students must use media center and computer lab time efficiently; they must stay focused on their research questions.

2. Evaluate information critically and competently: Students will determine if the information is up to date and if the source is likely to be biased or unbiased.

3. Use information accurately and creatively: Students will be creating charts, graphs and tables from their information, as well as doing basic statistical analysis (mean, median, mode, quartiles) as appropriate.

4. Pursue information related to personal interests by selecting a county with some personal relevance.

5. Appreciate literature and other expressions of information: fiction, biography, autobiography, travel accounts, and historical fiction may all provide information for this project.

6. Strive for excellence in information seeking and knowledge generation.

7. Recognize the importance of information to a society: Students will be acting as demographers, county planners, and school planners when they make predictions based on their data.

8. Practice ethical behavior in regard to information and information technology: Students will properly cite all sources used, follow copyright laws, and practice ethical behavior online and in the media center.

Figure 8.4. (Continued)

Technology Literacy Skills

1. Pre-requisite computer skills: basic computer, keyboarding, word processing and Internet navigation skills, computer lab procedures and etiquette . . .
2. Computer skills to be taught or reviewed
   a. Excel spreadsheet: setting up a data table, creating a chart, adding a trend line
   b. Word processing: inserting Excel tables and charts into word processing documents
3. Calculator skills
   a. Basic TI-83+ operations
   b. Creating various plots using tables and STAT PLOT function
   c. Graphing functions using y=
   d. Linear, quadratic and exponential regression, and graphing those functions
   e. Pasting TI-83+ graphs into Word documents

Resources

o Trade books (travel guides, fiction set in Georgia, biographies of Georgians)
o Library books on Georgia history and geography, encyclopedias, almanacs, atlases, road atlases
o Social studies and algebra textbooks
o Newspapers
o Magazines (*Southern Living,* travel magazines, regional magazines)
o County publications (Chamber of Commerce brochures, travel and tourism brochures, economic development information)
o State and federal government publications
o Genealogy resources
o Internet resources (census information, county school district information, Chamber of Commerce/tourism Web sites, college Web sites, corporate Web sites, etc.)

Technology

o TI-83+ graphing calculators
o Computers (word processing, printing graphs from calculators, spreadsheet, graphics, research)
o Digital photography
o Digital video

Teacher Responsibilities:

Algebra Teacher

o Teach mathematical skills, graphing skills, calculator use, and spreadsheet use
o Create specific math assignments for the project, such as
   • create circle graphs relating to demographic data
   • create timelines showing major events in the county's history

Figure 8.4. (Continued)

- create bar and line graphs for other county data, generate mathematical models from the graphs
- collect and analyze actual data from an "e-pal" 8th grade class, perhaps comparing it to our class
- explore the county's population growth or decline and the social or economic factors that caused the changes
- predict future population by creating mathematical models based on census data
- create math word problems based on information about the county

o Collaborate with social studies teacher on joint assignments
o Collaborate with media and technology specialists
o Provide instruction in research process as described above
o Conference with students
o Create Web site with information resources

Social Studies Teacher

o Provide instruction in research process as described above
o Collaborate with algebra teacher on joint assignments
o Collaborate with media and technology specialists

Media Specialist

o Create "Pathfinder" help sheet with resources listed
o Assist students in locating print and online resources
o Monitor research in media center

Technology Specialist / Technical Support Specialist

o Keep the computer labs running and Internet available
o Monitor research in computer labs

Student Responsibilities:

o Complete assignments in a timely manner
o Use Internet resources responsibly
o Conduct research efficiently and effectively
o Create appropriate products for each assignment
o Reflect on each assignment and on the overall project

Student Evaluation Rubric:

Example: When the algebra class covers making circle (pie) graphs, the County Project assignment will be to locate some data about your county that would be appropriate to display using a circle graph. This data could be related to population, industry, agriculture, education, or whatever

Figure 8.4. *(Continued)*

other topic the student locates that is appropriate. For this project, the rubric would be something like:

category	4–5 points	6–7 points	8–9 points	10 points	Score
data selected is appropriate to type of graph	graph attempted, but not appropriate to the data	circle graph created, but not appropriate (data not fractions of whole)	circle graph is acceptable, but another graph would be better	circle graph is most appropriate for the data	
data: accurately represented, source identified	major problems with accuracy and source incorrectly identified (i.e., "Google" instead of www.blairsville.com)	some problems with accuracy and source partially identified, cannot be verified	graph seems accurate but source data not provided. source is correctly identified, but incorrect form	source data is provided, graph is accurate source is correctly identified using correct bib. form	
graph: labels	no labels	missing title or legend, or legend says "series 1"	title and/or legend not descriptive, more labels needed	descriptive title, legend and other labels	
graph: good design and layout principles	poor layout and design	graph does not fit on page, or printed on spreadsheet. Name may be missing	graph needs design work, student name missing	graph attractive, fits on page, student name	
reflection	minimal reflection, less than one sentence	one or two sentences, or no evidence of actual thought	good ideas, but too short; or long enough, but no actual thought.	minimum one good paragraph reflecting on the process	
				Total Score (out of 50)	

Figure 8.4. *(Continued)*

Designer reflection on this process

During the school year, I tried several new strategies with my students, including having them create their own algebra word problems based on anything in the state of Georgia, tying in with their social studies curriculum of Georgia history and geography. Several students chose to look at population growth in various Georgia counties and create scatter plots or line graphs from the population data, as we had seen similar problems in the algebra textbook. We then carried this activity a step further, again following the algebra curriculum, and attempted to find the line-of-best-fit and an equation that would describe the data. It became quickly obvious that the linear equations the students were familiar with at that point were insufficient. Some of the population changes could best be described with more complex functions that these students would not explore until later in the year. In the spring, after the students were familiar with exponential functions, we revisited the population data and the students were better able to create mathematical models to describe their data. At that time I also asked them to apply what they knew about Georgia and speculate as to why the population changes occurred.

This led me to thinking about how else the social studies curriculum could be tied into the algebra curriculum, and the Georgia Counties Project was born.

This project will enhance student learning by providing real-life uses for the skills they learn in algebra class which should improve their understanding of both algebra and the State of Georgia. Students will be asked to use higher-order thinking skills to compare and contrast their selected county with our county in many of the projects. This analysis, and their creation of original graphs, charts, and equations, should direct them away from the copy-paste approach to information-gathering and lead them into drawing their own conclusions and doing original research.

<u>References </u>[for the unit]

Eighth Grade Academic Knowledge & Skills 2005–2006. (2005). Lawrenceville, GA: Gwinnett County Public Schools.

Jackson, E. (2005). Georgia Counties. Retrieved June 30, 2005 from <u>http://www.cviog.uga.edu/Projects/gainfo/county.htm</u>

COMMENTS ON THE GEORGIA COUNTIES COLLABORATIVE PROJECT

This unit cleverly combines two high school curriculum content areas not normally considered for an interdisciplinary unit: algebra and social studies. I-Search strategies (webbing, topic choice, pre-notetaking, creating questions) provide motivating interest for the year-long unit. Traylor and colleagues use the I-Search *pre-search* strategies to design and enhance learning activities that use algebra and social studies cognitive tools to explore authentic settings. These strategies serve as the initial structure and organization for increasingly complex use of research information converted to mathematical displays. Having already taught a unit with the goal to tie mathematics assignments to an authentic Georgia county setting, Traylor and colleagues redesign the unit to include a tightly structured *pre-search* process that ensures students will have interesting social studies data to create the mathematical displays.

The social studies teacher and media specialist's responsibilities are especially strong at this point in the unit. Because the students work on this project over the school year, Kathy and colleagues include strategies that create student interest and motivation to carry out the unusual and sophisticated assignments. After becoming acquainted with the I-Search components, Kathy Traylor includes I-Search strategies that allow the design of a total curriculum unit package that crosses disciplines and fulfills her teaching and learning goals. Other colleagues in the school who want to use the unit will tweak the unit design for their own teaching and learning goal responsibilities within the unit.

On the CD-ROM included with this book, you will find additional units that University of Georgia students have graciously agreed to share, including several for elementary and primary levels.

Use of I-Search reading/writing/research strategies to enhance student learning growth appears limited only by imagination. Certainly the Traylor unit is a prime example of using I-Search strategies for a strong, interdisciplinary project in a discipline, not noted for research projects, combined with a discipline for which research is a frequent assignment. This unit is an example of creativity in responding to curriculum and information literacy standards. It is an excellent model for imagining a unit design that will cover research standards via a full I-Search or an inclusion of one or more strategies that enhance student learning. If you do not force the strategies into an artificial situation, your students will respond by demonstrating a higher level of learning, thinking, writing, and reading for information use.

In the final two chapters of this book, the authors discuss the I-Search as a strong process for enhancing reading skills. The I-Search will enhance effectively the "No Child Left Behind" Act reading requirements.

REFERENCES

Duncan, D., and Lockhart, L. (2000). *I-search, you search, we all learn to research*. New York: Neal-Schuman.

Eisenberg, M. B., and Berkowitz, R. E. (1988). *Curriculum initiative: An agenda and strategy for library media programs*. Norwood, NJ: Ablex.

9 CONNECTING I-SEARCH TO READING

Beginning in 2001, school media specialists faced the challenge of accountability as outlined in the No Child Left Behind (NCLB) Act, a reauthorization and revision of the Elementary and Secondary Education Act. The I-Search, as adapted in this book, melds strategies through the process approach that connect the Act's three critical areas of reading, research, and writing. The I-Search strategies for teaching information literacy utilize reading and writing strategies throughout the I-Search assignment.

A Department of Education pamphlet summarizes the NCLB goals: "Under No Child Left Behind, every state has these mandates:

- Set standards for grade-level achievement and
- Develop a system to measure the progress of all students and subgroups of students in meeting those state-determined grade-level standards." (*A Guide to Education and "No Child Left Behind,"* 2004, p. 22).

One of the tenets of the act is the measurement of individual schools against a rating scale for "Adequate Yearly Progress" (AYP), meaning yearly proficiency improvements in national test scores. Unfortunately, the U.S. Department of Education's explanation of AYP is confusing. Each state can contribute its own explanation in describing schools' responsibilities as charged by the act. The Texas Education Agency (2005) presents a reasonable explanation:

> Under the accountability provisions in the No Child Left Behind (NCLB) Act, all public school campuses, school districts, and the state are evaluated for Adequate Yearly Progress (AYP). Districts, campuses, and the state are required to meet AYP criteria on three measures: Reading/Language Arts, Mathematics, and either Graduation Rate (for high schools and districts) or Attendance Rate (for elementary and middle/junior high schools).
>
> If a campus, district, or state that is receiving Title I, Part A funds, fails to meet AYP for two consecutive years, that campus, district, or state is subject to certain requirements such as offering supplemental education services, offering school choice, and/or taking corrective actions.

Moreover, each year greater percentages of students must meet the level of proficiency outlined in state standards in reading and

> The I-Search utilizes reading and writing strategies throughout the process.

math. All students must be proficient by 2013–2014. Instruction in the I-Search process, as outlined in this book, would contribute strongly to achievement growth in reading by virtue of the reading strategies learned, their use, and integration in the process.

Another key term related to NCLB, "scientifically based research" (SBR), must be a designation on any program that schools adopt to meet their AYP goals. An ERIC Digest provides a basic definition for SBR that defines it as: "*persuasive* research that *empirically* examines *important questions* using *appropriate methods* that ensure *reproducible and applicable findings*" (Beghetto, 2003, para 9). SBR programs have to be based on valid research methodologies, and pass a rigid peer review by experts. They cannot be fads. Reviews of current programs, projects, and practices in use can be found on the What Works Clearinghouse page: http://www.whatworks.ed.gov/.

How does the I-Search assignment meet the criteria for an SBR program? The answer is in a pamphlet accessed from the National Institute for Literacy Web site: "Put reading first: The research building blocks for teaching children to read" (CIERA, 2003). The pamphlet reviews current research on reading and summarizes the findings of the National Reading Panel, a group of experts mandated by Congress to review and analyze the research on reading. It also makes practical suggestions for applying the research. Within the pamphlet is the link between the I-Search methodology and proven strategies for teaching vocabulary and reading comprehension.

A review of recommended, research-based strategies for teaching reading comprehension justifies the teaching of the I-Search process in the age of NCLB. The National Reading Panel experts identify six proven strategies that support comprehension:

> I-Search methodology links to proven strategies for teaching vocabulary and reading comprehension.

1. monitor comprehension (includes metacognition, i.e., thinking about thinking),
2. use graphic and semantic organizers,
3. answer questions,
4. generate questions,
5. recognize story features, and
6. summarize (CIERA, 2003 pp. 56–59).

> The I-Search process embeds reading comprehension strategies in a number of tools.

The I-Search process embeds the recommended strategies for teaching and improving reading comprehension in the following I-Search process tools, thus making the I-Search an excellent process for teaching students how to read informational texts. The connection between the recommended reading strategies and I-Search strategies is as follows:

Figure 9.1. Template: Connection Among Reading Strategies	
Recommended Strategy	**I-Search Process Tools**
Monitoring (includes metacognition)	Double-Entry Drafts, Learning Logs
Using Graphic and Semantic Organizers	Webbing
Answering Questions	Pre-Notetaking Sheet, Conferencing, Learning Logs
Generating Questions	Pre-Notetaking Sheet, Double-Entry Drafts
Recognizing Story Structure [text features]	Making Meaning of Text through Double-Entry Drafts
Summarizing	Double-Entry Drafts, Learning Logs

MONITOR COMPREHENSION

According to the CIERA document (2003), "Students who are good at monitoring their comprehension know when they understand what they read and when they do not. They have strategies to 'fix up' problems in their understanding as the problems arise" (p. 55).

Double-entry drafts and learning logs are effective tools for monitoring reading because they call for the application of metacognition needed for comprehension monitoring. Students use the content column of double-entry drafts to record confusing passages and unfamiliar words. The response column becomes an area for restating the passage in their own words or using context clues to speculate on word meanings. You can assist in the monitoring and "fix up" process by encouraging your students to use the following strategies:

> Double-entry drafts and learning logs assist students in utilizing metacognition for reading comprehension.

- identify where the difficulty [in comprehension] occurs,
- identify what the difficulty is,
- restate the difficult sentence or passage in their own words,
- look back through the text, and
- look forward in the text for information that might help them to resolve the difficulty. (CIERA, 2003, p. 56)

Students use learning logs as places to reflect on the strategies they use to monitor their reading and repair problems in understanding.

Learning logs become a place for reflecting on the strategies students use to monitor their reading and repair problems in understanding. These strategies strengthen comprehension and contribute to student achievement.

GRAPHIC AND SEMANTIC ORGANIZERS

The scientifically based research on reading and work with the I-Search process reveals that graphic and semantic organizers are powerful, visual tools for increasing comprehension of texts. In fact, the pre-notetaking sheet used to activate prior knowledge and generate research questions is a modified version of a graphic organizer called a KWL chart. The use of research questions increases students' ability to read for comprehension by providing a purpose for reading. Activating prior knowledge, *what I know,* helps students to link new information to past experience and learning, thus increasing comprehension.

Reading comprehension improves when students use essential questions to focus their reading.

You will find it effective to use a variety of graphic organizers to help students understand specific texts and compare and/or contrast texts. For example, students use webbing and spider diagrams to represent visually the main ideas and supporting details within a text. They use charts and Venn diagrams to compare/contrast information from two texts. Many templates and ideas for using graphic organizers are available on the Internet. In addition to templates, students love creating graphic organizers using computer programs.

Graphic and semantic organizers assist understanding and comparing and/or contrasting information in texts.

Graphic and semantic organizers are powerful tools for young I-Searchers. As the CIERA (2003) Partnership for Reading document notes, graphic organizers:

- help students focus on text structure as they read;
- provide students with tools they can use to examine and visually represent relationships in a text; and
- help students write well-organized summaries of a text. (p. 57)

Tools and techniques embedded within the I-Search process help students learn and practice scientifically based reading strategies.

ANSWER AND GENERATE QUESTIONS

A strong link among I-Search techniques and scientifically based reading strategies connects to generating and answering questions, a focus of the scientifically based research, which lies at the heart of a successful I-Search. Not only does the pre-notetaking sheet help students generate questions to guide the search and find a focus, but it also facilitates reading comprehension by activating students' prior knowledge.

The research concludes that answering questions provides these benefits:

- gives students a purpose for reading,
- focuses students' attention on what they are to learn,
- helps students to think actively as they read,
- encourages students to monitor their comprehension, and
- helps students to review content and relate what they have learned to what they already know. (p. 57)

> The pre-notetaking sheet helps students generate questions to focus their research.

The pre-notetaking sheet accommodates this strategy by having students complete a *what I know* column. Students further elaborate on their prior knowledge in their learning logs. Developing vocabulary is another aspect of prior knowledge. Part of the pre-notetaking process includes background reading that helps students fill in gaps in prior knowledge and understand the vocabulary associated with their topics.

Answering questions is another important strategy for improving reading comprehension. You assist students in selecting personally meaningful research topics as students complete their interest webs. Then you pose questions that help students articulate what they know about their topics and how their topics relate to their lives. During peer conferences, students ask their friends to explain their topics, give further details about their knowledge of the topic, and justify the choice of topic. Answering questions motivates students to want to read by connecting their topics to a specific need for information and to their past experiences.

Questions posed by media specialists and their collaborating partners during conferences further enhance reading comprehension. As noted in the CIERA document, questions "prompt an understanding of information that is":

> Peers and teachers ask students questions to help them articulate what they know and what they should find out about their topics.

- text explicit (stated explicitly in a single sentence),
- text implicit (implied by information presented in two or more sentences), or

- scriptal (not found in the text at all, but part of the reader's prior knowledge or experience). (p. 57)

While conferencing or responding to student double-entry drafts and learning logs, pose questions that help students clarify their purpose for reading. Ask questions that help students monitor their comprehension, repair errors in interpretation, and compare/ contrast information from a variety of resources.

Generating questions is the key to the *pre-search* phase of the I-Search process, when students generate questions to guide their search and find a focus. They use the pre-notetaking sheet, both the draft and revision, to brainstorm what they do not know about their topics. They use generic questions from Bloom's *Taxonomy* and other models to create new, higher-order questions. From this question generation, they select the four or five related questions to guide their search under an umbrella of an essential question. These questions also provide a purpose for reading and facilitate comprehension.

Making meaning of the text in the I-Search allows for the inclusion of the following steps:

- survey the text,
- predict the content,
- relate the predicted content to prior knowledge,
- interact with the text, and
- reflect on the content.

If you want to strengthen your students' reading comprehension, you can show them how to preview by skimming and scanning the article, paying special attention to the title, first and last paragraphs, information in bold print or italics, graphics (e.g., charts, graphs, photographs, and drawings), and abstract—when available. Have them preview to create a list of key words and concepts related to the text. Then ask them to predict the content by using the key words and concepts to generate a list of potential questions that might be answered in the text.

Before reading the text for details, students activate their prior knowledge. They determine what questions they can answer from their prior learning and speculate on answers to the remaining questions. Once they generate questions and relate them to their prior knowledge, they read the text looking for the answers to their questions. In addition, they note key words and concepts not covered in their preview. The final step involves reflection as they summarize what they have learned by answering their questions. They also use metacognition to describe their learning

> Ask questions that help students monitor their comprehension, repair errors in interpretation, and compare/contrast information.

> The I-Search strategies prompt students to survey their texts, predict content, relate to prior knowledge, interact with the text, and reflect on how the content informs their questions.

process, explain how they overcome obstacles encountered while reading the text, and note successful strategies to apply to future reading assignments. Asking and answering questions lies at the heart of making meaning of the text.

RECOGNIZING STORY STRUCTURE

Text features aid in comprehension. Show students how different text types (e.g., bold print, italics) signal key concepts or vocabulary. Model how headings and subheadings contribute to their understanding of main ideas and supporting details and how bullets highlight lists of significant details. Discuss how charts, graphs, illustrations, photographs, and sidebar articles interact with text to give meaning. Have your students practice these steps in reading text to integrate the ways that text features and the structure of information texts improve reading comprehension.

SUMMARIZATION

Summarizing information texts is another key to understanding. According to scientifically based research, summarizing

> is a synthesis of the important ideas in a text. Summarizing requires students to determine what is important in what they are reading, to condense this information, and to put it into their own words. (CIERA, 2003, p. 59)

Double-entry drafts and learning logs provide an excellent tool for summarizing and making meaning of a text.

USING READING STRATEGIES TO SCAFFOLD A CURRICULUM CONTENT AREA I-SEARCH

The I-Search is an ideal process for teaching the key, scientifically based reading strategies. But what does this look like within the curriculum? One example of the successful application of these reading strategies occurred during a content area I-Search on constitutional law, a collaborative unit designed and implemented by media specialist Marilyn Joyce and social studies teacher Alice Thomas at Brewer High School in Brewer, Maine. The unit reveals how educators modify the I-Search to meet the demands and time constraints of content area instruction.

Joyce and Thomas's unit planning follows the backward design process outlined by Wiggins and McTighe (1998) in *Design for Understanding*. They use three stages in their planning:

- identify the desired results,
- determine the acceptable evidence, and
- plan learning experiences and instruction. (p. 9)

The first stage in the collaborative planning process necessitates the articulation of essential learning suitable for high school juniors in American history. The primary goal of the unit is to evaluate the effectiveness of the Constitution as a vehicle for change, one of Maine's history standards. Their "curricular priorities" list begins with the big ideas represented by "enduring understanding." These consist of the state and national standards to be addressed in the unit. The items under "important to know" refer to concepts and processes needed to achieve enduring understanding. Meanwhile, the "worth being familiar with" concept refers to the basic vocabulary and facts that provide the background knowledge that forms the foundation for understanding what students will read and view (Wiggins and McTighe, 1998, pp. 9–10).

Enduring Understandings
- To understand how and why the Constitution changes and adapts over time; and
- To "evaluate the effectiveness of the Constitution as a vehicle for change" (Maine Learning Results, 1997)

Important to Know
- To apply the judicial review process to a specific case
- To explain how the legal precedents contribute to the court's decision
- To explain how the social and political climates influence the court's decision and predict what will happen in the future

Worth Being Familiar With
- To summarize the majority and minority opinions for the court case

- To list the court cases that provide the legal precedents and summarize the court's opinion on each
- To explain the legal terminology associated with the cases (e.g., "clear and present danger," "cruel and unusual punishment," "symbolic speech")

To accomplish these goals, students will research a Supreme Court case and share their findings with peers through oral presentations.

"Acceptable evidence" of learning success involves selecting assessments "to document and validate that the desired learning has been achieved" (Wiggins & McTighe, 1998, p. 12). Joyce and Thomas decide to replace the pre-notetaking sheet with other activities and assessments because the questions students will use to guide their searches are predetermined by the state history content standards.

The double-entry draft is a perfect tool for students to demonstrate their understanding of the facts, vocabulary, concepts, and processes found under "important to know and do" and "worth being familiar with." The double-entry drafts will also reveal problems in understanding concepts and ideas.

Conferencing allows them to intervene when necessary. Finally, the learning log is an assessment tool for tracking the items under "enduring understandings." Having a plan of action for determining the acceptable evidence, these strategies help Joyce and Thomas create their lessons and activities.

First, Joyce and Thomas design an activity to introduce the assignment. Joyce knows from her work with Jeffrey Wilhelm, a literacy specialist at the University of Maine, that students need a frontloading activity. Frontloading is "a way to prepare, protect, and support students into the acquisition of new content and ways of doing things. Frontloading is the use of any prereading strategy that prepares students for success" (Wilhelm, Baker, & Dube, 2001, p. 92). They start the unit with the following survey as an introductory activity to stimulate thinking, activate prior knowledge, and emotionally connect students to the topic of judicial review.

> The double-entry draft scaffolds student understanding of facts, vocabulary, concepts, and processes informing their essential question.

Figure 9.2. Sample: Constitutional Law Student Survey

Constitutional Law: A Survey

Would you fight for the following . . .

1. To use whatever quotation you want under your yearbook picture?
2. To wear political buttons or T-shirts supporting a candidate or cause?
3. To express your true feelings on a controversial issue (e.g., abortion, gay rights), even if the opinion is politically incorrect?
4. To organize a prayer group for students and pray in school?
5. To wear a T-shirt advertising alcohol or displaying drugs?
6. To include language deemed "unacceptable" in a composition written for creative writing class?
7. To refuse to take a drug test in order to participate in sports or other co-curricular activities?
8. To prohibit the use of drug-detecting dogs in the school?
9. To publish frank articles in the school newspaper on controversial issues such as teen pregnancy and contraception?
10. To keep your library records private?

Both teachers have students share responses in small discussion groups and report out on the findings.

Joyce and Thomas also anticipate potential problems relating to schema or "the rich set of understandings around a particular topic" (Wilhelm, Baker, & Dube, 2003, p. 97). They want to know, "What do students know about the court system?" What if students have misconceptions about judicial review? Instead of using a pre-notetaking sheet, they decide to activate students' prior knowledge by having them respond to the following writing prompt in their learning logs: "What do you know about the court system (criminal court, civil court, and the Supreme Court) and how do you know it—from school, the media, personal experience, or stories from friends?"

> Ask students to probe questions to identify their prior knowledge gaps.

Student responses to these probe questions help Joyce and Thomas identify gaps in prior knowledge. They find out that their students have a good deal of prior knowledge of the criminal court system based on their viewing of television shows and movies. Some follow famous criminal cases on Court TV and in the newspapers. But their knowledge of the Supreme Court seems minimal. Thomas wonders if her students would be able to distinguish between criminal courts that emphasize guilt or innocence and the Supreme Court that focuses on the interpretation of the law.

They decide to fill in the gaps in prior knowledge and develop the necessary vocabulary by having their students view portions of a video about *Brown v. Board of Education*. Thomas plans a lesson in which students view the scenes where the case is argued before the court and where the Justices debate the issue in chambers. During the viewing, students keep a double-entry draft. In the content column, students record their observations about Supreme Court procedures and in the response column they comment on what they learn, note confusing elements, and pose questions. A homework assignment follows where students answer these questions in their learning logs:

- What process is used by the Supreme Court to interpret the law?
- What role do the Justices play?
- How is the Supreme Court different from civil or criminal courts?
- In general, what do you now know about the how the Supreme Court interprets the law?

Joyce and Thomas use the learning logs as an assessment tool. They check the logs for accuracy and intervene when students express confusion or lack the necessary understanding to proceed with the assignment. They answer questions posed by students. Sometimes their intervention takes the form of a mini-lesson for the entire class. Individual interventions include one-on-one conferencing and responding to student double-entry drafts and learning logs.

Content area I-Searches sacrifice a degree of topic choice in order to cover curriculum. Nevertheless, it is possible to provide choice and encourage students to select personally meaningful topics. To accomplish this task, students receive a list of possible court cases, each with a one-sentence summary of the issue covered in the case. Then students have access to resources, books, and recommended Web sites, and time for background reading. Students use these resources to select cases that arouse their curiosity and motivate them to continue reading about the case.

Due to time constraints, Thomas provides students with preconstructed questions to guide their search. The questions and probes for responding to them appear in the form of a double-entry draft template to serve as a model for the structure the teachers want the students to use.

> While curriculum content area I-Searches necessarily sacrifice a degree of topic freedom, it is still possible to provide enough topic choice to identify personally meaningful topics.

Figure 9.3. Sample: The Supreme Court and the Enduring Constitution

The Supreme Court and the Enduring Constitution

Citation:

Content	Response
1. Court case and date • A summary of the case • An explanation of the court decision (majority and minority)	1. Possible responses • Explanation of text: Put a passage from the text in your own words. Explain why the information is important. Why did you pick that information? • Personal reactions: Do you agree or disagree with the decision? How do you feel about the issue? What side are you on and why? • Emerging questions: What new questions come to mind? (E.g., if a black arm band is acceptable, why can't I wear a shirt with a beer logo?) • Connections between the court case and a current or past controversy
2. Legal precedents • A summaries of the cases • An explanation of the court decisions (majority and minority)	2. How do the precedents contribute to the outcome of your case? Has the interpretation of the Constitution changed? If there is a change in the Court's point of view on the issue, what is the cause (social or political) of the change?
3. Cases that follow and dates • A summary of the case • An explanation of the court decision (majority and minority)	3. How do the precedents contribute to the outcome of your case? Has the interpretation of the Constitution changed? If there is a change in the Court's point of view on the issue, shat is the cause (social or political) of the change?

For this assignment, the double-entry drafts give Joyce and Thomas opportunities to pinpoint errors in interpretation of text and facilitated conferencing. After selecting topics, Thomas's classes spend several periods in the library gathering resources and taking notes using the DED template. Thomas and Joyce use the time to review and conference with students about their work.

Reading strategies and tools provide the scaffolding and support for the content area I-Search on Constitution Law. By the end of one unit, students felt so comfortable using and talking about reading strategies that they even modified one of the I-Search tools to meet their personal learning needs. Several students struggling with the language of the Court decisions dealt with the problem by modifying the format of the double-entry draft into a triple-entry draft. They inserted a column between their content and response to use as a space for paraphrasing key passages from the Court's decisions noted in the content column. For these students, the I-Search provided a structure that encouraged troubleshooting problems related to reading comprehension.

Although the Supreme Court unit is a partial I-Search with adapted strategies, it illustrates how media specialists and their partner teachers can modify the I-Search process to meet the needs of content area learning. Most importantly, it shows how scientifically based reading strategies can be integrated into a content area I-Search.

> Reading strategies and tools frequently provide the scaffolding and support in curriculum content areas I-Searches.

CONCLUSION

> "Good readers have a purpose for reading" (CIERA, 2003, p. 54).

The I-Search process creates an environment for successful comprehension instruction by establishing a personally meaningful purpose for reading, which facilitates active reading by motivating students to solve their problems, make informed decisions, and investigate topics that arouse their curiosity. Most importantly, the I-Search process provides a framework for teaching and practicing successful, research-based strategies for improving reading comprehension. Think about the I-Search process as more than a framework for teaching research. A successful I-Search unit is packed with instruction and practice in the six key reading strategies outlined in scientifically based research, as reported in the *Put Reading First* document (2003). In the age of NCLB, our graduate students wonder if they have the time to teach the I-Search process. The answer is a resounding "yes!"

Who is responsible for teaching students how to read information texts? Many content area teachers feel unprepared to teach reading strategies. This, then, is an excellent opportunity for the library media specialist, the expert in information literacy, and the content area teachers to get involved in collaboratively planning an I-Search-enhanced unit that answers those needs. Knowledge of the six strategies for improving reading comprehension and the I-Search strategies makes the library media specialist ideally situated for co-teaching students how to read information texts. Through collaboratively planned I-Search units, library media specialists and content area teachers teach students textual comprehension strategies, a key step to achieving the goals of NCLB.

The authors have added new strategies, new connections to content areas, and an understanding of the relationship between reading for comprehension and the I-Search process. The narrative voice for this book addresses you, the reader, directly. The intent is to describe the I-Search process prescriptively for more clarity in structure and strategies. The authors have taught I-Search units for a number of years now, and each time they gained more understanding of the process. As a result, they developed new strategies that move the I-Search process into another dimension.

The first edition contained very little material on the I-Search in the content area, and this edition remedies this. Readers ask continually, "How does the I-Search work in content area units?" Very well, indeed. Chapter 8 includes an example of the I-Search in an eighth-grade algebra and social studies interdisciplinary unit that integrates much of the I-Search process. The comments by the designer reveal her planning techniques and how she thinks the unit will improve the existing unit. Although this unit is mainly the design of the algebra teacher, Kathy Traylor, she enlists her colleagues' planning advice, suggestions, and support before they co-teach with her, helping her create the final agenda for the unit. You will find other I-Search units, including at the elementary level, on the accompanying CD-ROM. These units could serve as models for a full or partial I-Search in the content area.

Because the authors have examples of adult I-Searches from students, you will find actual I-Search products at the high school and adult levels on the CD-ROM. The differences will be striking but, at the same time, similar in process and storytelling. You will sense the high level of motivation and interest in their writing through their topic ownership. Yes, the I-Search takes careful planning and time for the unit. However, read the result in the quality of research and writing that these papers demonstrate.

> Knowledge of the six strategies for improving reading comprehension, as well as the I-Search strategies, situates the media specialist ideally to co-teach students how to read information texts.

> This chapter includes new strategies, new connections to curriculum content areas, and an understanding of the relationship between reading for comprehension and the I-Search process.

The result of all the I-Search strategies combined is a research, writing, and reading process that is adaptable to whatever needs the students have, as long as they retain ownership of their topics.

The value of all the I-Search strategies combined into a research, writing, and reading process is their adaptability to whatever needs the students have, as long as the students retain ownership of their topics and learn the strategies essential to filling their needs. When they do not have topic choice, rarely do they own the topic once they research it. Once students learn how to develop a relationship with their topic and discover their interest in their topic, they develop and satisfy a personal hunger for understanding through their I-Search. They invest in their research.

When processes interweave, they gain strength from each other and provide students with a stronger foundation for achievement as an information-literate person. Instead of teaching processes, individual research steps, or individual skills isolated from their connections to writing and reading, the I-Search connects all three. The I-Search provides a natural exposure to strategies that help students solve their problems and answer their questions, whether in the classroom or in life outside the classroom.

The I-Search is an inquiry research process based on the information processing theory of learning and intimately connects with other critical learning processes taught in reading and writing classes. If you are a process teacher and advocate, you will find it fits naturally into your instructional plans. If you have not followed process teaching, take the time to integrate one or more of the strategies into your current units and examine how they affect student learning growth. Be patient with your units and build on them each year. It is worth the investment for the research, writing, and reading foundation it gives students as they complete their studies.

REFERENCES

Beghetto, R. (2003). "Scientifically based research." *ERIC Digest*, 167. Retrieved December 25, 2004, from http://eric.uoregon.edu/publications/digests/digest167.html

Center for the Improvement of Early Reading Achievement (CIERA). (2003). *Put Reading First: The Research Building Blocks of Reading Instruction*, 2nd ed. Partnership for Reading. Retrieved August 19, 2005, from http://www.nifl.gov/partnershipforreading/publications/Cierra.pdf

National Reading Panel. (2000). *Teaching children to read*. Retrieved December 25, 2004, from http://www.nationalreadingpanel.org/

Partnership for Reading. "Questions about reading instruction." Retrieved December 28, 2004, from http://www.nifl.gov/partnershipforreading/questions/questions_about.html#comprehension

Renstrom, P. G. (1992). *Constitutional law for young adults*. Alexandria, VA.: ABC-CLIO.

State of Maine. (1997). "Learning results document." Augusta, ME: State of Maine. Retrieved August 19, 2005, from http://www.elm.maine.edu/mlr/ mlr4.asp?ContentArea=Social+Studies&Standard=C.++FUNDAMENTAL +PRINCIPLES+OF+GOVERNMENT+AND+CONSTITUTIONS& TableName=Social&StandardArea=CIVICS+AND+GOVERNMENT &Grade=Secondary+Grades&Go=Go

Texas Education Agency. (2005). *Adequate yearly progress (AYP)*. Retrieved August 19, 2005, from http://www.tea.state.tx.us/ayp/

United States Department of Education. Office of the Secretary. Office of Public Affairs. (2004). *A guide to education and 'No Child Left Behind.'* Washington, DC: U.S. Department of Education. Retrieved August 20, 2005, from http://www.ed.gov/nclb/overview/intro/guide/guide.pdf

United States Department of Education. Institute of Education Sciences. *What works clearinghouse*. Retrieved January 2, 2005, from http:// www.whatworks.ed.gov/

Wiggins, G. & McTighe, J. (1998). *Understanding by design*. Alexandria, VA.: Association for Supervision and Curriculum Development.

Wilhelm, J. D., Baker, T. N., & Dube, J. (2001). *Strategic reading: Guiding students to lifelong literacy 6–12*. Portsmouth, NH: Boynton/Cook.

Part III
I-Search Resources

ANNOTATED BIBLIOGRAPHY: SELECTED REFERENCES

Abilock, D. (2003). *NoodleTeach: Teaching intelligently*. Retrieved August 20, 2005, from http://www.noodletools.com/debbie/ Noodle Tools is a rich teachers' Web site primarily developed by Debbie Abilock, editor of the American Association of School Librarians' professional journal, *Knowledge Quest*. This page contains links to thoughtful articles on literacy and curriculum collaboration.

Atwell, N. (1987). *In the Middle*. Portsmouth, NH: Heinemann. Describes Atwell's experience teaching process writing to middle school students. Provides insight into the nature of the process approach to teaching.

Beghetto, R. (2003). "Scientifically based research." *ERIC Digest*, 167. Retrieved December 25, 2004, from http://eric.uoregon.edu/publications/digests/digest167.html Defines and gives a history of scientifically based research. Presents anticipated implications for school leaders.

Bloom, B. S. (1974). *Taxonomy of educational objectives: The classification of educational goals*. New York: D. McCay. This reprint of the original describes a hierarchy of critical thinking skills which has guided teachers and media specialists in the creation of student learning experiences and the assessment of student progress.

Bowen, C. (2001). "A process approach: The I-Search with grade 5: They learn!" *Teacher Librarian, 29*(2), 14–18. Discusses I-Search process unit taught at fifth grade level, and its affect on motivation, and outcome.

Breivik, P. S. and Gee, E. G. (1989). *Information literacy: Revolution in the library*. New York: American Council on Education/Macmillan. Shows the movement from information skills to information literacy in library instruction.

California Media and Library Educators Association. (1994). *From library skills to information literacy: A handbook for the 21st Century*. Castle Rock, CO: Hi Willow Research and Publishing. Contains an excellent definition of information literacy.

Call, P. E. (1991). "SQ3R + what I know sheet = On strong strategy." *Journal of Reading, 35*(1), 50–54. Describes how to combine SQ3R and a variation of the pre-notetaking sheet to improve reading skills.

Callison, D. (2000). *Key instructional term: Motivation*. Retrieved August 1, 2005, from http://www.crinkles.com/keyWords.html Discusses the need for motivation to ensure successful teaching and learning.

Callison, D. (2003). "Models: Part V composition models." *School Library Media Activities Monthly, 19*(5), 34–37. Discusses several research models including the I-Search.

Center for the Improvement of Early Reading Achievement. (2003). *Put reading first: The research building blocks of reading instruction*. 2nd ed. Partnership for Reading. Retrieved August 19, 2005, from http://www.nifl.gov/

partnershipforreading/publications/Cierra.pdf Summarizes the findings of the National Reading Panel's review of scientifically based research on reading. Features a reader-friendly format.

Chow, C. and Members of the Washington Library Media Association Supervisors' Subcommittee Information Skills. (1987). *Information skills curriculum guide: Process, scope, and sequence.* Olympia, WA: Washington Office of the State Superintendent of Public Instruction. (ERIC Document, ED288554.) Contains the research process model adopted and modified by Maine Educational Media Association's Ad Hoc Committee on Information Skills in its *Information Skills Guide for Maine Educators* (see citation below).

Collins, P. J. (1990). "Bridging the gap." In Atwell, N. (ed.) *Coming to Know: Writing to Learn in the Intermediate Grades* (pp. 17–31). Portsmouth, NH: Heinemann. Describes a process approach to teaching resource-based writing with sixth graders. Contains excellent student models.

Davis, J. M. (1997). *I-Search paper.* Retrieved August 20, 2005, from http://teachers.net/lessons/posts/80.html Posted on the "teachers.net" Web site which is set up as a database of curriculum units in a variety of content areas. Davis has written a letter explaining the I-Search project to parents and students, giving activities, expectations, and due dates during the assignment. Organized and structure approach to informing students and parents about the I-Search assignment.

Dellinger, D. G. (1989). "Alternatives to clip and stitch: Real research and writing in the classroom." *English Journal, 78*(5), 31–38. Describes a collaborative learning project using the I-Search paper. Has model assignments and procedure sheets. Shows how surveys and interviews are used to gather information.

Doll, C. (2003). "Ken Macrorie's I-SEARCH MODEL." *School Library Media Activities Monthly, 19*(6), 24, 3p. Doll discusses the I-Search model and its application in K–12 education connected with the developmental levels of learners.

Downie, S. L. (1988). "Ethics, a choice for the future: An interdisciplinary program." *English Journal, 78*(5), 28–30. Focuses on using the I-Search to analyze controversial issues. Information gathering strategies include use of guest speakers, interviews with experts, and field trips.

Duncan, D. and Lockhart, L. (2000). *I-Search, you search, we all learn to research: A how-to-do-it manual for teaching elementary school students to solve information problems.* New York: Neal-Schuman. Excellent worksheet templates for an I-Search unit at the elementary level.

Duncan, D., and Lockhart, L. (2005). *I-Search for success.* New York: Neal-Schuman. Thorough presentation of an elementary grade level I-Search unit, providing planning directions and strategies.

Eisenberg, M. B. and Berkowitz, R. E. (1988). *Curriculum initiative: An agenda and strategy for library media programs.* Norwood, NJ: Ablex.

Eisenberg, M. B., and Berkowitz, R. E.. (1993). *Information problem-solving: The Big Six Skills approach to library and information skills instruction.* Norwood, NJ: Ablex. Describes how to implement the "Big Six" skills across the curriculum. Another model of the research process.

Eisenberg, M. B. and Brown, M. K. (1992). "Current themes regarding library and information instruction: Research supporting and research lacking." *School Library Media Quarterly, 20*(2), 103–109. Contains a summary of research findings and a list of questions for further research. Includes the following themes: the value of library and information skills instruction, the nature and scope of library and information skills, and the integrated approach. Contains comparison chart of information skills process models.

Emig, J. (1971). *The composing process of twelfth graders.* NCTE Research Report No. 13. Urbana, Ill.: National Council of Teachers of English. One of the early research studies on process writing.

Garland, K. (1995). "The information search process: A study of elements associated with meaningful research tasks." *School Libraries Worldwide, 1*(1), 41–53. Summarizes the results of a study investigating what makes a good research task. The five elements contributing to satisfaction with the research process and satisfaction with achievement are (1) student choice of topic, (2) group work, (3) course-related topics, (4) clarity of goals and means of evaluation, and (5) process instruction.

Guidelines for drafting your I-Search reflection. Retrieved August 20, 2005, from http://www.bcpl.net/~sullivan/modules/tips/i-search/reflguide.html Slightly different way of addressing organization of I-Search paper. Useful as a checklist for adaptation to use with students.

Harada, V. H. (2002). "Personalizing the information search process: A case study of journal writing with elementary-age students." *School Library Media Research, 5.* Retrieved August 20, 2005, from http://www.ala.org/ala/aasl/aaslpubsandjournals/slmrb/slmrcontents/volume52002/harada.htm A study of journal writing in the elementary grades "as a means of deepening students' cognitive and affective awareness of the information-search process."

Holt, John. (1983). *How children learn.* Rev. ed. New York: Da Capo Press.

Irving, A. (1985). *Study and information skills across the curriculum.* London: Heinemann. Presents the philosophy behind the process approach to teaching information skills and gives one of the first models of the research process.

Joyce, M. Z. (1995). "The I-Search paper: A vehicle for teaching the research process." *School Library Media Activities Monthly, 11*(6), 31–32, 37. Provides an overview of the I-Search process.

Joyce, M. Z. (1998). "Preparing students for the information age through the I-Search process." *KLIATT 32(2),* 2–5. Presents a case study of a high school student's I-Search project.

Kaszyca, M., and Krueger, A. M. (1994). "Collaborative voices: Reflections on the I-Search project." *English Journal, 83*(1), 62–65. Describes an I-Search project for high school students which integrates literary research with peer support.

Kuhlthau, C. C. (1987). "An emerging theory of library instruction." *School Library Media Quarterly, 16*(1), 23–28. Traces the evolution of library skills instruction from the "source approach" through the "pathfinder approach" to today's "process approach."

Kuhlthau, C. C. (1989). "Information search process: A summary of research and implications for school library media programs." *School Library Media Quarterly, 18*(1), 19–25. An explanation of Kuhlthau's model of the information search process.

Kuhlthau, C. C. (1993). *Seeking meaning: A process approach to library and information services.* Norwood, NJ: Ablex. Summarizes Kuhlthau's research resulting in her model of the Information Search Process.

Kuhlthau, C. C. (1995). "The process of learning from information." *School Libraries Worldwide, 1*(1), 1–12. Presents the process approach to teaching information literacy as the key concept for the media center in the Information Age.

Macrorie, K. (1988). *The I-Search paper.* Rev. ed. Portsmouth, NH: Heinemann. The original source of the I-Search. Proposes an alternative to the traditional research paper.

Maine Educational Media Association's Ad Hoc Committee on Information Skills. *Information skills guide for Maine educators.* (1990). Augusta, ME: Maine State Library. A curriculum guide containing the thirteen-step research process used in this book. Contains student objectives and suggests strategies for implementing stages of the research process.

Maine Educational Media Association's Information Skills Committee. *A Maine sampler of information skills activities for Maine student book award nominees, 1992–1993.* (1993). Augusta, ME: Maine State Library. Contains a chart of Bloom's Taxonomy and corresponding action words used to generate questions and create activities for students at different levels in their thinking. The taxonomy is frequently used as an assessment tool for evaluating students' critical thinking skills.

Make it happen: The I-Search unit. Retrieved August 20, 2005 from http://www.edc.org/FSC/MIH/i-search.html. A powerhouse site full of relevant links to student learning and the I-Search. Worth exploring in depth for explanations and strategies for teaching the I-Search.

Maxim, D. (1990). "Beginning researchers." In Atwell, N. (ed.). *Coming to know: Writing to learn in the intermediate grades* (pp. 3–16). Portsmouth, NH: Heinemann. Describes a process approach to teaching resource-based writing with third graders. Contains excellent student models.

McKenzie, J. (n.d.). *FNO.ORG From now on: The Educational Technology Journal.* Retrieved August 20, 2005, from http://www.fno.org. Jamie McKenzie writes and edits this electronic journal which is packed with constructivist, student-centered ideas for teachers and media specialists.

Merriam-Webster's Collegiate Dictionary. (2003). 11th ed. Springfield, MA: Merriam-Webster.

Mitchell, S. P. (1988). "Before the search: Genuine communication and literary research." *English Journal, 78*(5), 46–49. Applies the I-Search to an author study. Emphasizes pre-search strategies and use of student journals to generate and interpret ideas.

Murray, D. M. (1982). "Writing as a process: How writing finds its own meaning." In Murray, D. M. *Learning by teaching: Selected articles on writing and teaching.* (pp. 17–31). Portsmouth, NH: Heinemann. An excellent introduction to the idea of writing as information processing.

National Reading Panel. (2000). *Teaching children to read.* Retrieved December 25, 2004, from http://www.nationalreadingpanel.org/. Presents the findings of a panel convened by Congress to evaluate the effectiveness of different approaches to reading instruction.

Nicolini, M. B. (1999). "Pictures of an exhibition: Senior graduation exit projects as authentic research." *English Journal, 89*(1), 91–98. A yearlong I-Search project that high school seniors undertook as a capstone project, culminating in a presentation to a panel of school community adults they did not know.

Olson, C. B. (comp.). (2000). *Practical ideas for teaching writing as a process at the high school and college levels.* Rev. ed. Sacramento, Calif.: California State Department of Education. Discusses writing process models, techniques, and strategies.

Partnership for Reading. *Questions about reading instruction.* Retrieved December 28, 2004, from http://www.nifl.gov/partnershipforreading/questions/questions_about.html#comprehension. Presents FAQs on the five essential elements of reading instruction: phonemic awareness, phonics, fluency, vocabulary, and comprehension.

Rankin, V. (1988). "One route to critical thinking." *School Library Journal, 34*(5), 28–31. Describes a process approach to research used with middle school students.

Rankin, V. (1992). "Pre-Search: Intellectual access to information." *School Library Journal, 38*(3), 168–179. Describes a method for teaching the pre-search stage of the research process to middle school students.

Rankin, V. (1992). "Rx: Task analysis or, relief for the major discomforts of research assignments." *School Library Journal, 38*(11), 29–32. Suggests strategies for helping students with judging the suitability of resources, comprehending information, and evaluating and extracting information.

Redding, N. (1994). "Assessing the big outcomes." In Kuhlthau, C. C. (ed.). *Assessment and the school library media center.* (pp. 131–136). Englewood, CO: Libraries Unlimited.

Renstrom, P. G. (1992). *Constitutional law for young adults.* Alexandria, VA: ABC-CLIO. Used as a resource for social studies units on Supreme Court cases.

Rubin, B. C. (2002). "Beyond 'I': Critical literacy, social education, and the "'I-Search'." *Penn GSE Perspectives on Urban Education, 1*(2), 1–21. 9th grade I-Search unit in a social issues course. I-Search project enhanced literacy skills.

State of Maine. (1997). *Learning results document.* Augusta, ME: State of Maine. Retrieved August 19, 2005, from http://www.elm.maine.edu/mlr/mlr4.asp?ContentArea=Social+Studies&Standard=C.++FUNDAMENTAL+PRINCIPLES+OF+GOVERNMENT+AND+CONSTITUTIONS&TableName=Social&StandardArea=CIVICS+AND+GOVERNMENT&Grade=Secondary+Grades&Go=Go Lists State of Maine standards and performance indicators for civics.

Stripling, B. K. (1995). Learning-centered libraries: Implications from research. *School Library Media Quarterly, 23*(3), 163–170. Contains an excellent section on authentic assessment.

Stripling, B. K. and Pitts, J. M. (1988). *Brainstorms and blueprints: Teaching library research as a thinking process.* Littleton, CO: Libraries Unlimited. Contains a model of the research process which stresses the development of critical thinking skills. Describes a variety of activities for teaching the process.

Tadlock, D. F. (1978). "SQ3R—why it works, based on an information processing theory of learning." *Journal of Reading, 22*(2), 110–112. Explains the reading strategy SQ3R and relates it to information processing.

Tallman, J. I. (1995). "Connecting writing and research through the I-Search paper: A teaching partnership between the library program and classroom." *Emergency Librarian, 23*(1), 20–23. A summary of the process steps used in a ninth grade I-Search experience. Contains student anecdotes.

Tallman, J. I. (1995). "Helping students to construct their own learning: The I-Search and student-directed learning as a research experience." *Learning and Media, 23*(3), 10–11. Summarizes a Maine freshman English class experience with the I-Search.

Tallman, J. I. (1998). "I-Search: An inquiry-based, student-centered, research and writing process." *Knowledge Quest, 27*(1), 20–27. Discusses the I-Search research process from an inquiry-based approach.

Texas Education Agency. (2005). *Adequate yearly progress (AYP)*. Retrieved August 19, 2005, from http://www.tea.state.tx.us/ayp/. Provides one state's interpretation of Adequate Yearly Progress under No Child Left Behind.

United States Department of Education. Institute of Education Sciences. *What works clearinghouse*. Retrieved January 2, 2005, from http://www.what works.ed.gov/. Reviews educational programs, products, practices, and policies using the standards of scientifically based research.

United States Department of Education. Office of the Secretary. Office of Public Affairs. (2004). *A guide to education and "No Child Left Behind."* Washington, D.C.: U.S. Department of Education. Retrieved August 20, 2005, from http://www.ed.gov/nclb/overview/intro/guide/guide.pdf. Presents a user-friendly summary of the No Child Left Behind Act.

University of Victoria. Counselling Services. (2005). *Learning skills program: Bloom's Taxonomy*. Retrieved August 20, 2005, from http://www.coun.uvic.ca/learn/program/hndouts/bloom.html. Adapted from Benjamin S. Bloom. (1984). *Taxonomy of educational objectives*. Boston, MA: Allyn and Bacon (with permission of publisher). Explains each level of the Taxonomy and gives an excellent list of question cues for each level.

Web English Teacher. (2005). *Writing research and I-Search papers*. Retrieved August 20, 2005, from http://www.webenglishteacher.com/research.html. Links to several research and writing sites for the I-Search.

Where do I stand? An I-Search rubric. Retrieved August 20, 2005, from http://www.bcpl.net/~sullivan/modules/stand/intro/isrub.html. A self-assessment student marking rubric for the I-Search paper.

Wiggins, G., and McTighe, J. (1998). *Understanding by design*. Alexandria, VA: Association for Supervision and Curriculum Development. Presents a framework for curriculum development based on standards and authentic assessment.

Wilder, S. (2005). "Information literacy makes all the wrong assumptions." *Chronicle of Higher Education, 51*(18), B13.

Wilhelm, J. D., Baker, T. N., and Dube, J. (2001). *Strategic reading: Guiding students to lifelong literacy 6–12*. Portsmouth, NH: Boynton/Cook. Describes numerous reading strategies designed to move students into higher-level texts.

Wilson, H. A. and Castner, F. (1999). "From Mickey Mouse to Marilyn Manson: A search experience." *English Journal, 89*(1), 74–81. Describes the I-Search process through Gardner's multiple intelligences lens.

Yanushefski, J. (1988). "The biography: The research project as literary discourse." *English Journal, 78*(5), 50–58. Describes how to write a biography of a living person using the I-Search format.

Yell, M. M. (1999). "Multiple choice to multiple rubrics: One teacher's journey in assessment." *Social Education, 63*(6), 326–29. Discusses writing assessments through rubrics for response notebooks and the I-Search essay.

Zirinsky, D. (1995). "'How long does it have to be?' Helping our students understand research writing." *Word works: Learning through writing at Boise State University, (72)*. Retrieved August 20, 2005, from http://www.boisestate.edu/wcenter/ww72.htm. Electronic journal article addresses student research complaints as well as describes some of the major I-Search attributes, such as topic ownership.

Zorfass, J. M. (1998). *Teaching middle school students to be active researchers.* Alexandria, VA: Association for Supervision and Curriculum Development. Geared to middle school educators, this book describes the I-Search and its components in detail with appendices that include planning and assessment criteria.

Zorfass, J. M. and Dorsen, J. (2002). "ScienceQuest: Literacy development within an informal science education initiative." *Reading Online, 5*(7). Retrieved August 20, 2005, from http://search.epnet.com/login.aspx?direct=true&db=eric&an=EJ669373. Discusses ScienceQuest, which is an informal program in which young adults meet to study science phenomena using I-Searches.

Zorfass, J. M., and Giguere, P. J. (1996). *Make it happen! Search organizer.* Newton, MA: Education Development Center. A looseleaf binder with a 10-minute video providing teaching strategies for the I-Search centered on the elementary age group.

INDEX

ABOUT THE AUTHORS

Julie I. Tallman, Ph.D., Professor, Department of Educational Psychology and Instructional Technology, The University of Georgia, teaches in the Department's school media program for Master's, Ed.S., and Ph.D. students. Her most prized teaching memories are of the lifetime impact that personal I-Searches have had on some of her students. Prior to becoming a university professor, Julie had years of professional teacher-librarian experience at middle school through university level. A Fulbright Senior Scholar at the University of Botswana in 1999–2000, Julie has also taught the I-Search process in Botswana, the Republic of South Africa, and New Zealand.

Marilyn Z. Joyce, M.L.S., M.A., is a former secondary school English teacher. She is teacher-librarian at Brewer High School in Brewer, Maine, and an online adjunct instructor for the University of North Texas School of Library and Information Sciences. Marilyn is a member of the Advisory Committee for the Laura Bush Foundation and has served on the Planning Committee for the 2009 revision of National Assessment of Educational Progress in Reading.